The United States COAST GUARD

A PICTORIAL HISTORY

The United States
COAST GUARD
A PICTORIAL HISTORY

By Gene Gurney

Foreword by Admiral C. R. Bender
Commandant, U.S. Coast Guard

Crown Publishers, Inc. New York

Inquiries should be addressed to Crown Publishers, Inc., 419 Park
Avenue South, New York, N.Y. 10016
Library of Congress Catalog Card Number: 72-84304
ISBN: 0-517-50099X
Printed in the United States of America
Published simultaneously in Canada by General Publishing Company
Limited

Art Direction: Michael Perpich
Design: Carol Callaway

Acknowledgments

I wish to thank the following persons at the United States Coast Guard Headquarters for their kind, courteous, and professional help in putting this volume together: Captain J. H. Durfee, USCG, Chief, Office of Public and International Affairs, and his Chief Yeoman L. W. Zens, USCG; Captain T. McDonald, USCGR, Chief, Public Affairs Division; Captain Berry L. Meaux, USCG, Assistant Chief, Public Affairs Division; Mr. James R. Ward, Community Relations Director; Lieutenant Commander Gilbert Shaw, USCG, Chief Media Relations Branch; Mr. Harold E. Whitwer, Chief, Visual Services Branch (who in World War II was the photographer of some of the photos contained in this book); Chief Warrant Officer Joseph Greco, USCG, Assistant Press Officer, Public Media Branch; Chief Warrant Officer Kendal J. Parsons, USCG, Assistant Chief, Visual Services Branch; USCG Photojournalists James Hammond, Tamotsu Nakata, and James Whalen; and the Coast Guard's project officer for the book, the USCG Historian, Truman Strobridge.

The contemporary photographs were provided through the courtesy of the United States Coast Guard, and the historical photographs through the courtesy of the National Archives and Records Service. I am particularly grateful to Miss Elizabeth A. Segedi, Photo Editor, Public Affairs Division, United States Coast Guard, who achieved some miraculous finds in coming up with special photos for the book; and I wish to thank James W. Moore, Chief, Audio-Visual Records, National Archives and Records Service, for making available to me the U.S. Coast Guard's retired photographs and records.

Gene Gurney

Contents

ADMIRAL C. R. BENDER

Foreword

Since its beginnings in 1790 as a revenue fleet of ten small cutters, the U.S. Coast Guard has constantly evolved over the years through the acquisition of new responsibilities. Today, besides being the foremost federal agency for maritime safety and marine law enforcement, the U.S. Coast Guard engages in such diverse activities as search and rescue, aids to navigation, military readiness, port security, boating safety, ocean stations, icebreaking, and oil pollution control.

In addition, although essentially a humanitarian Service, dedicated to saving life and property at sea, the U.S. Coast Guard is no stranger to warfare. As the nation's oldest continuous seagoing Service, it has seen combat alongside the other military services in the many conflicts of the United States ranging from the quasi-war with France in the late eighteenth century to the recent conflict in Vietnam. Until 1967, the U.S. Coast Guard served within the Treasury Department. At present, it is part of the Department of Transportation. The Coast Guard is part of the Armed Forces at all times and operates as part of the U.S. Navy in time of war or when the President so directs.

The U.S. Coast Guard's operations, despite the Service's name, are global in nature, stretching from the Arctic to the Antarctic regions and from shores of Europe to Southeast Asia. The Service today has come a long way since the first Secretary of the Treasury, Alexander Hamilton, sponsored its first ten cutters off the eastern coast of North America.

This book tells both in text and pictures the important story of the U.S. Coast Guard and its multifaceted activities over the years. This is a field of history too often neglected by the American maritime and military writer. In writing the first pictorial history of the U.S. Coast Guard, Gene Gurney has provided a valuable historical reference work. It should be of interest not only to Coast Guardsmen and their families, but to all persons interested in this unique humanitarian military Service.

ADMIRAL C. R. BENDER
Commandant, U.S. Coast Guard

Alexander Hamilton, the first Secretary of the Treasury, whose proposal for a "system of Revenue Cutters" led to the founding of the organization that became the United States Coast Guard. Photographed from a painting by C. L. Ransom, which hangs in the office of the Secretary of the Treasury, Washington, D.C.

Boats for Securing the Collection of the Revenue

In July of 1789 the United States government was only a few months old. A president, vice-president, and a congress had been elected and the legislative process had begun. New York City was the nation's temporary capital. It would be another eleven years before the government moved to a new Federal City on the Potomac River.

In New York President George Washington and the Congress struggled with the many problems that threatened the continued existence of the infant republic. One of the most pressing of these problems was money. The national debt totaled well over fifty million dollars and revenues could only be described as inadequate.

Necessity dictated that one of the first pieces of legislation considered be an attempt to improve the country's finances and Congress quickly passed a protective tariff that imposed duties on the tonnage of vessels and on "goods, wares and merchandizes imported into the United States." The Tariff Act authorized "Customs surveyors" for the country's ports and "the employment of boats which may be pro-

vided for securing the collection of the revenue."

While Congress may have contemplated a fleet of boats to assist in collecting import duties, it failed to provide the money to pay for them. Meanwhile, up and down the east coast citizens were discovering that it was possible to bring imported goods ashore without paying the new duties.

In 1789 there were many Americans who did not consider smuggling to be a crime. Indeed, only a few years earlier smuggling had been regarded as an act of patriotism. Before the Revolutionary War, when the British had attempted to tax molasses, sugar, wine, glass, lead, paints, paper, tea, and other products imported by the colonies, the Americans had complained loudly of taxation without representation and refused to abide by the British king's trade regulations. Merchants in port towns signed nonimportation agreements and the ordinary citizen depended on the ubiquitous smuggler to keep him supplied with tax-free goods.

Smuggling continued during the Revolution as the Americans used their familiarity with the se-

Launched in 1791, the MASSACHUSETTS was the first and the largest of the original ten revenue cutters. The vessel remained in service until 1798 when she was sold. Photographed from a painting by Hunter Wood.

cluded harbors and inlets along the Atlantic coast to evade the patrolling ships of the British Navy. The smuggler was a respected individual and his business was a profitable one. More often than not, he continued to do some "importing" after the coming of peace and the organization of the new United States government. As a result, customs collectors handled only a portion of the taxable goods coming into the country and the Tariff Act of 1789 failed to produce the expected revenue.

Congress had anticipated this problem when it recommended a fleet of boats to aid in collecting import duties, and George Washington's able Secretary of the Treasury, Alexander Hamilton, agreed with the legislators. In a report on the operations of the Tariff Act submitted to Congress in April, 1790, he wrote that the boats were indeed necessary if the Tariff Act was to be enforced.

Hamilton had already contacted the Treasury's collectors of customs on the subject of boats. "I shall be glad to have your ideas on the expediency of employing them in your quarter," he wrote in a circular letter, "and (if they appear to you necessary) of the number and kind you deem requisite, their armament and probable expense."

In his report to Congress Hamilton outlined the plan he had worked out for a fleet of revenue cutters. The Secretary wanted ten boats: "two for the coasts of Massachusetts and New Hampshire; one for Long Island Sound; one for New York; one for the Bay of Delaware; two for the Chesapeake (these to ply along the neighboring coasts); one for North Carolina; one for South Carolina; and one for Georgia."

According to Hamilton, such a fleet, completely equipped, could be acquired for ten thousand dollars. Annual operating expenses were estimated at $18,560. The Secretary proposed paying the ships' captains $40 a month and other officers $25. Seamen were to draw $8. Provisions for the fleet would cost $3,000 a year, and wear and tear would add another $2,000 to operating expenses. But, Hamilton pointed out, the ten boats were sure to add more to the revenue than they cost.

Perhaps to forestall a Congressional attempt to economize on wages, Hamilton defended his pay scale. He told the legislators: "The utility of an establishment of this nature must depend on the exertion, vigilance, and fidelity, of those to whom the charge of the boats shall be confided. If these are not respectable characters, they will rather serve to screen, than detect fraud. To procure such, a liberal compensation must be given, and, in addition to this, it will, in the opinion of the Secretary, be advisable that they be commissioned as officers of the navy. This will not only induce fit men the more readily to engage, but will attach them to their duty by a nicer sense of honor."

After due deliberation, Congress, now meeting in Philadelphia, gave Hamilton his ten boats with the provision that the ten thousand dollars needed to purchase them must come out of customs duties collected by the Treasury Department. The enabling legislation referred to the vessels as "Revenue Cutters," a term that is still in use today.

But Congress disregarded Secretary Hamilton's advice on crews for the Treasury's cutters. The Congressmen stipulated that each cutter was to have a master; a first, second, and third mate; four mariners, or sailors, and two boys. Masters were to receive $30 a month and the subsistence of an Army captain. Pay for first mates were set at $20 a month. Second mates were to get $15 and third mates $14, with all mates receiving the subsistence of Army lieutenants. A soldier's subsistence went to the mariners and boys who were to draw $8 and $4 a month, respectively.

Congress further stipulated that once the cutters were in operation, officers of the customs could board any ship arriving in the United States or entering waters within four leagues of the coast en route to the United States. The boarding officers were authorized to search the ships, certify their manifests, and secure hatches and other communications with hold areas. They were to remain with the ships until they docked.

Alexander Hamilton asked his collectors of customs to help him arrange for the building of the revenue fleet. In a letter to Benjamin Lincoln, the collector at Boston, he recommended a large cutter for the Massachusetts coast. "The want of a few tons in the burthen will often occasion loss of revenue, and on some trying occasions may prove fatal to the vessel herself, and the lives of those on board her," he wrote. Mindful of the sorry state of the country's finances, the Secretary cautioned: "Render the cost as moderate as possible."

The need for the strictest economy "consistent with the safety and comfort of officers and men and the effectual execution of the public service" was a theme that recurred in Hamilton's correspondence with the collectors. He recommended the purchase of domestic sailcloth, which he considered a better buy than cloth imported from England, and proposed placing a large order with a Boston manufacturer. "The largeness of the quantity will enable and induce the owners of the factory to supply it on the most reasonable terms," he wrote.

Searle and Tyler of Newburyport, Massachusetts, received the first of the cutter contracts. It was for the two-masted schooner *Massachusetts* at an estimated cost of $23.50 a ton. Apparently the cutter program quickly ran into the same cost overrun problems that were to plague government procurement in later years. Secretary Hamilton found it necessary to suggest that the *Massachusetts* be reduced from 64 tons if it could be done safely. The cutter under construction at New York was to be only 35 tons and the one on the ways at Hampton, Virginia, would measure 47 tons and both were considered safe and efficient, he advised Boston Collector Lincoln, who was supervising the building of the *Massachusetts*. Moreover, the Secretary opined, it might be advisable to omit one of the boats planned for the *Massachusetts* "and such other things as can be spared in supplies and furnishing."

In spite of Hamilton's proposed economies, Searle and Tyler found that their expenses for building the *Massachusetts* ran some $600 over the contract price, another harbinger of things to come.

Collector Lincoln disclaimed all responsibility. He had warned the builders about making any changes that would increase costs. But at the request of John Foster Williams, the newly appointed master of the *Massachusetts,* Searle and Tyler had added 17 tons to the ship's size and installed "a handsome head and quarter badges, and a considerable carved work about her stern."

To avoid a loss on the *Massachusetts,* Searle and Tyler proposed replacing it with a smaller vessel, a suggestion that Secretary Hamilton allowed might be acceptable to the Treasury Department. But in the end the *Massachusetts* took up station off the coast of the state whose name she bore.

Measuring 50 feet from Indian figurehead to stern, the first Treasury cutter was an imposing vessel. Her beam was 17 feet, 8 inches: her hold depth, 7 feet, 3 inches. The ship's final weight was 70½ tons.

Nine more cutters soon joined the *Massachusetts* in guarding the coast against smugglers. They were the 51-ton *Scammel,* patrolling off New Hampshire; the 50-ton *Active* and 50-ton *Pickering,* in Chesapeake Bay; the 40-ton *Diligence,* off North Carolina; the 35-ton *Argus,* in Long Island Sound; the 35-ton *Vigilant,* off New York; the 35-ton *Virginia,* assigned to Virginia waters; the 35-ton *South Carolina,* to intercept shipping bound for that state, and the 30-ton *General Greene,* in Delaware Bay. The *Massachusetts* carried six swivel guns whose revolving bases allowed them to be turned in any direction. The *General Greene* had three guns and the others had four guns apiece.

While the cutters were under construction, Secretary Hamilton turned his attention to recruiting. John Foster Williams, the man he chose to command the *Massachusetts,* was a veteran of the Continental Navy as were the *Active*'s commander, David Porter, and Hopley Yeaton, commander of the *Scammel.* Yeaton's commission as a "Master of a Cutter in the Service of the United States," signed by George Washington, is the only one of the original commissions still in existence. All cutter officers took an oath to support the Constitution and to prevent and detect frauds against laws of the United States imposing duties upon imports.

Another of the original cutters, the 50-ton PICKERING, was named for Postmaster General Timothy Pickering, a friend of Alexander Hamilton.

GEORGE WASHINGTON, President of the United States of America.

TO ALL WHO SHALL SEE THESE PRESENTS, *GREETING*.

KNOW YE, That reposing special Truft and Confidence in the Integrity, Diligence and good Conduct of *Hopley Yeaton of New Hampshire* . . . . I DO APPOINT him *Master* . of a Cutter in the Service of the United States, for the Protection of the Revenue; and do authorize and empower him to execute and fulfil the Duties of that Office according to Law; AND TO HAVE AND TO HOLD the said office, with all the Rights and Emoluments thereunto legally appertaining, unto him the said *Hopley Yeaton* . . during the Pleasure of the President of the United States for the Time being.

IN TESTIMONY whereof I have caused these Letters to be made Patent, and the Seal of the United States to be hereunto affixed. GIVEN under my Hand, at the City of *Philadelphia*, the *Twenty first* . Day of *March* . in the Year of our Lord one thousand seven hundred and ninety *one*, and of the Independence of the United States of America the *Fifteenth*.

G. Washington

By the President

Th. Jefferson

On March 21, 1791, President George Washington signed the commissions of the first thirteen officers appointed to serve on the ten revenue cutters then under construction. The commission of Hopley Yeaton, the only one still in existence, is reproduced here.

What little information is available suggests that the first officers of the customs dressed much as the officers of the Continental Navy dressed before it was disbanded in 1785. Ship's masters probably wore blue swallow-tailed coats with gold buttons, boots, and cocked hats over hair tied up in short queues. Buttons, arranged in groups of four on lapels, pocket flaps, cuffs, and coat skirts, indicated the rank of sea captain. Officers wore side arms and carried speaking trumpets which they used to call orders to the crew and to hail other ships.

Sailors, who were called mariners in those days, wore short blue jackets with brass buttons and bell-bottomed trousers that could be either rolled up or worn over boot tops. Hair hung in pigtails that were tarred for protection against the weather. For dress a mariner donned a hard black hat with a flat brim and a pillbox crown. At sea he wore a knitted cap.

Alexander Hamilton's determination that the revenue cutters succeed in their mission led him to offer detailed advice to the newly commissioned officers of the customs as they prepared to take up their duties. In a circular letter dated June 4, 1791, he recommended that they make extensive patrols of the coasts in the neighborhood of their stations. To remain in one place, he pointed out, would defeat the purpose of the revenue cutters since it would allow "fraudulent practices" everywhere else.

In the Secretary's opinion, American ship masters had been given enough time to become acquainted with the provisions of the tariff laws. "It is now indispensable that they should be strictly enforced," he told his customs officers. He suggested that they keep a careful watch on small coasting vessels to prevent the unloading of goods before a ship arrived in port, "one of the most extensive cases of illicit trade," according to Hamilton. However, they should not challenge a vessel unless there were good reasons for doing so. He advised boarding when inbound vessels carried high-duty or valuable cargo, when they carried quantities of easily removable goods on deck, and in other suspicious circumstances, the boarding party to remain with the vessel until she docked.

Counseling activity, vigilance, and firmness marked with prudence, moderation, and good temper, Hamilton noted: "On these last qualities, not less than the former, must depend the success, usefullness, and consequently continuance of the establishment."

When they took to the sea in 1791, the Secretary of the Treasury's "boats" had no official name. Congress had referred to the vessels as revenue cutters and it gave the title "officer of the customs," to the men in charge of the cutters. Hamilton, in his request to Congress, had proposed a "system of Revenue Cutters." Other early documents refer to the Revenue Cutter Service, the Revenue Service, the Revenue Marine, and the Revenue Marine Service. An 1863 statute refers to the United States Revenue Cutter Service, but this name continued to be used interchangeably with Revenue Marine Service until 1894 when Revenue Cutter Service became the accepted designation of the organization we now know as the United States Coast Guard. Well before its last name change, however, Alexander Hamilton's proposal for a system of revenue cutters had proved its value over and over again.

Defenders of the Nation's Coasts

While there is no official record of the smuggling operations thwarted by the first Coast Guardsmen, the fact that in 1793 Congress voted to raise the pay of the eighty men who crewed the Treasury's ten cutters may be an indication that they were doing a good job. Under the new pay schedule, captains received $40 a month; first lieutenants, $26; second lieutenants, $20, and third lieutenants, $18. Mariners received up to $10 a month. In 1796 Congress voted another pay increase for the cutter crews that raised a captain's wages to $50 a month. First lieutenants were raised to $35, second lieutenants to $30, third lieutenants to $25 and mariners to $20.

In spite of the pay increases some discipline problems troubled cutter operations. In one case, the third mate of the *Massachusetts* was dismissed for insulting Captain Williams, failing to pay proper respect to his superior officers while on board ship, speaking disrespectfully of them in public company, and "keeping bad women on board the Cutter in Boston."

Troublemakers, such as the *Massachusetts's* third mate, were an exception, however. By and large, the cutter crews were men of high caliber who had a difficult job to do and did it well. A steady increase in customs receipts in the years after 1791 attests to their success.

Unfortunately, Alexander Hamilton's ten cutters proved to be unsuited to the task they were expected to perform. The Secretary's economies may have been necessary to win the approval of Congress for the purchase of ten cutters, rather than five or six, but the resulting vessels were too small and undermanned to keep the nation's coasts and harbors under constant surveillance. In 1795 Hamilton obtained Congressional permission to build a fleet of larger cutters, and by 1801 the Treasury's original ten revenue cutters had been replaced by thirteen new ships. Some of the new vessels were given the names of the cutters they replaced, beginning a custom that was to continue to the present day. The replacement program was not yet completed, however, when the revenue cutters were called upon to help defend United States interests in an undeclared war with France.

Privateers and men-of-war belonging to both Great Britain and France frequently attacked American shipping in the years of unrest that followed the Revolutionary War. In 1794 Jay's Treaty, named for Chief Justice John Jay, who handled the negotiations for the United States, temporarily settled the difficulties between Great Britain and her former colonies, but the attacks by French vessels continued. At first the United States, lacking a navy, did little to protect its ships and sailors. There was an American fleet available, however: the Treasury's revenue cutters, especially the larger, better armed new cutters. In 1797 Congress passed a law authorizing President John Adams to use revenue cutters to defend the coast and protect the country's commerce. If need be, he could increase a cutter's crew to thirty marines and seamen. But Congress cautioned that the cutter fleet must continue to enforce the Tariff Act while it carried out its additional duties.

For nine months, until Congress created a Navy Department in April, 1798, the revenue cutters served as the naval combat force of the United States, and some of the cutters continued their combat role after the Navy took to the seas. The *Pickering, Governor Jay, Eagle, Diligence, Virginia, General Greene, Scammel,* and *South Carolina,* with their crews, were transferred from the Treasury Department to the new United States Navy.

At first the revenue cutters assigned to naval duty were used chiefly to patrol coastal waters on the lookout for marauding French privateers because Congress had limited their combat activities to "defense against hostilities near the coast," although the cutters, carrying as many as ninety men and from ten to fourteen guns, compared favorably with the Navy's own vessels. In 1799, however, with the naval war spreading to the West Indies, Congress authorized President Adams to deploy the revenue cutters to full combat duty. Cutter crews were to receive Navy pay and subsistence and they were to be governed by Navy regulations. A second piece of legislation stipulated that in the future the Revenue Marine was to cooperate with the Navy whenever the President directed it to do so, a ruling that continues to apply to the present-day Coast Guard.

No longer confined to coastal duty, the *Governor Jay,* the *General Greene,* and the *Eagle* began cruising near Cuba. The *Pickering, Scammel,* and *Diligence* moved to Prince Rupert's Bay, the *Virginia* took up station off St. Kitts, and the *South Carolina*

This illustration of naval uniforms worn prior to the War of 1812 is based on a painting, one of the few sources of information about the uniforms of that period. Coats were blue, vests and breeches, buff.

patrolled in the Windward Passage. In their new combat stations they watched over the merchant ships that carried sugar, rum, and molasses from the West Indies to the United States and the ships bringing supplies to the Navy's West India Squadron.

Between 1798 and 1800, when the naval warfare ended, revenue cutters captured sixteen enemy ships. The most active of the cutters, the 187-ton *Eagle,* seized five, assisted in the capture of ten more, and retook seven American ships held by the French. Her sister ship, the *Pickering,* with a crew of seventy, defeated the *L'Egypte Conquise,* a heavily armed French privateer, after a battle that raged for nine hours. The privateer's crew had been increased to 250 men for the express purpose of capturing the *Pickering.* The *Pickering*'s prize was one of the biggest of the conflict. Unfortunately, her brave crew did not survive the undeclared war. In 1800 the *Pickering* was lost with all hands in a storm at sea.

The battle depicted here between the American ship PLANTER (right) and a French privateer raged for several hours on July 10, 1799, before the privateer was finally driven off. Such attacks on American vessels were the cause of the undeclared naval war with France.

With her guns blazing, the cutter EAGLE (left) is about to capture the French privateer MEHITABLE and the latter's prize, the NANCY, in one of the most famous engagements of the naval war with France.

Since 1799 a version of the Coast Guard ensign has flown on United States vessels engaged in enforcing maritime law as a symbol of their authority. An emblem, added to the seventh red stripe in 1910, assumed the form shown here in 1927.

Although the newest and largest of the Revenue Marine's cutters were serving with the Navy, enforcing the Tariff Act remained the Service's primary duty and in 1799 Congress authorized the cutters to display a distinguishing ensign as they patrolled the country's coast looking for smugglers. The Secretary of the Treasury in a letter to his customs collectors written in 1799 described the ensign: "16 perpendicular stripes, alternate red and white, the Union of the Ensign to be, the Arms of the U.S. in dark blue on a white field." The sixteen stripes stood for the sixteen states that then made up the United States. The original thirteen states were represented several times in the arms of the United States, by thirteen stars, thirteen arrows, thirteen leaves on the olive branch, and thirteen bars on the shield.

After 1910 the Revenue Cutter Service emblem appeared on the ensign, centered in the middle of the seventh red stripe. However, it was not until 1927 that the design of the emblem was officially designated as a shield within two concentric circles superimposed upon two anchors. Since then there have been only minor changes in the flag that flies from Coast Guard vessels as a mark of the organization's authority to enforce the marine laws of the United States, an authority that goes back to the 1799 ruling by Congress that stated: "Whenever any ship or vessel, liable to seizure or examination, shall not bring to, on being required to do so or on being chased by any cutter or boat, which has displayed the pendant and ensign prescribed for vessels in the Revenue Service, the master of such cutter may fire at, or into, such vessel, after such pendant has been hoisted and a gun fired by such cutter as a signal."

Although it had its own distinctive ensign, the Revenue Service soon found itself with fewer cutters from which to display it. Early in his presidency, Thomas Jefferson, who took office in 1801, reduced the number of cutters, their size, and the size of cutter crews. The trouble with France being resolved and smuggling on the decline, Jefferson questioned the value of the Treasury's fleet. He suggested that smaller ships, efficiently operated, ought to be able to protect the revenue.

In response to the President's wishes, his Secretary of the Treasury, Albert Gallatin, ordered some of the older cutters sold and smaller vessels commissioned to replace them. Meanwhile, in Europe, England and France had resumed hostilities and both nations were again interfering with American shipping. The belligerents instituted blockades and counterblockades that threatened the safety of American merchant vessels unless their masters complied with complicated rules. In addition, Great Britain insisted that American sailors were still British subjects and liable for service in the British Navy.

President Jefferson's solution to the problem was to ask Congress to prohibit American vessels from leaving the territorial waters of the United States. Congress passed the Embargo Act in 1807 and American shipping decreased drastically. It did not come to a complete standstill, however, because enterprising merchants found ways of evading the attempts of the Treasury's reduced cutter fleet to enforce the restrictive law.

Faced with a serious problem, Treasury Secretary Gallatin turned to Congress for help. He needed ten to twelve cutters, he told the legislators. They should range from 70 to 130 tons in size, carry from six to ten guns and be manned by fifteen to thirty seamen. The Secretary estimated that the vessels would cost from eight to twelve thousand dollars, exclusive of guns. Annual expenses were estimated at $108,000.

Congress, alarmed at the increase in illegal shipping, agreed to pay for twelve new cutters that the harried customs men so needed. In spite of their attempts to stop and search all suspected vessels,

An artist's conception of a cutter in 1800 shows the new Revenue Service ensign flying from the ship's mast.

This painting by an unknown artist shows a Revenue Service cutter (right) confronting a large English brig during the War of 1812.

American ships were regularly slipping off to West Indian and Canadian ports.

Within two years the Embargo Act had proved so difficult to enforce and so unpopular that Congress replaced it with new legislation permitting trade with all countries except France and England. This lightened the task of the men who manned the revenue fleet, but a new challenge lay ahead.

On June 18, 1812, the United States responded to continued harassment of American shipping by the British with a declaration of war on that country. Nine of the Revenue Marine's sixteen cutters immediately joined the Navy's combat force. Although the vessels were small, averaging 125 tons and carrying crews of fifteen to thirty men and six to ten guns, they acquitted themselves well in combat. The war was not yet a week old when the cutter *Jefferson* captured the *Patriot,* the first enemy ship to fall into American hands. Not long afterward, the cutter *Madison* took the 300-ton brig *Shamrock* as a prize. The *Madison* also captured the schooner *Wade,* which was carrying $20,000 in gold and silver. The *Dart,* a privateer that had taken more than twenty American ships, was herself captured by the cutter *Vigilant* after a daylong battle. In all, the cutters took fourteen enemy ships in spite of the fact that they were smaller and less heavily armed than most of the British vessels operating off the American coast. The cutters had been designed for speed, however, and they used it to good advantage.

Speed was not enough to save the cutter *Surveyor* when she was surprised by the British man-of-war *Narcissus* at the mouth of Virginia's York River. The *Narcissus* carried a crew of fifty compared with the *Surveyor*'s complement of fifteen. Undaunted by the odds against them, the men of the *Surveyor* fought desperately to defend their ship, using whatever weapons they could lay their hands on. They were finally forced to surrender, but not before they had killed three of the British boarders and wounded seven others.

As was customary, the defeated captain surrendered his sword to the victors. However, the British commander returned it the next day with a message in which he referred to "the sword you have so nobly used." He also expressed his admiration for the way the Americans had defended their ship "inch by inch." They had his wishes for a speedy exchange, the British commander assured the *Surveyor*'s captain.

Another Revenue Service cutter that the British captured after a gallant fight was the *Eagle.* She had sailed from New Haven, Connecticut, hoping to re-

The MADISON, shown here in a painting, scored an important naval victory for the United States when she captured the British brig SHAMROCK in 1812. A few months after her success, the MADISON was captured by the British near Savannah, Georgia.

take the American vessel *Susan* from an enemy force operating in Long Island Sound. Hampered by a lack of wind, the *Eagle* took a day to locate the *Susan,* now armed and protected by the eighteen-gun British ship *Dispatch.*

In order to escape the superior enemy force, the *Eagle*'s captain decided to beach his ship, which he did successfully under heavy fire from the *Dispatch.* The *Eagle*'s men quickly dismounted the grounded ship's guns and installed them at the top of a bluff. From there the besieged Americans returned the fire that the *Dispatch* was directing at them and at the abandoned *Eagle.* The *Eagle*'s crew continued the battle until their ammunition ran low, whereupon five cuttermen volunteered to return to the *Eagle* for more. Aboard the ship, with British shells bursting all around them, they replaced the *Eagle*'s ensign that had been torn away, collected some ammunition from the ship's stores and even salvaged shot from enemy guns that had lodged in the *Eagle*'s hull. Only three of the volunteers survived to return to the bluff. There they helped their crew mates use bits of cloth and pages from the *Eagle*'s logbook to make wadding for the rounds that the Americans fired at the British who were attempting to land to take the bluff. The counterattack forced the British to withdraw, and later the Americans were able to refloat the *Eagle*. But the *Dispatch* returned and this time she captured the damaged *Eagle*.

Taking note of the exploits of the men of the *Eagle, Jefferson, Vigilant, Surveyor,* and the other cutters, Congress, in 1814, voted to award cutter crews wounded or disabled while cooperating with the Navy the same pensions that were given to the officers and men of the Navy.

When the Treaty of Ghent brought the war with Britain to a close in December, 1814, the Revenue Service cutters that had survived the conflict resumed their patrol of the American coast. But now, in addition to smugglers, they were on the lookout for pirates and slave traders.

Pirates, based in the West Indies and in secluded harbors along the Florida and Louisiana coasts, were capturing merchant vessels, appropriating cargoes, and taking passengers and crews as prisoners. Merchantmen, only lightly armed or carrying no arms at all, were easy victims for the pirates who were especially bold and numerous in the Caribbean and the Gulf of Mexico.

Congress, concerned about the growing threat to American shipping, voted to protect the country's merchantmen with "armed public vessels." The armed public vessels turned out to be the cutters of the Revenue Marine. Wherever they patrolled, cutter crews were instructed to be on the lookout for suspicious vessels because pirate ships were apt to turn up anywhere.

Early in 1819 the customs collector at Baltimore reported an encounter with an audacious pirate crew. Their ship, a new schooner named *Hornet,* had been fitted out at Baltimore and the pirates had managed to slip out of the harbor "without the usual formalities." The collector's report continues: "The Revenue Cutter was sent after her and took possession of her whilst yet in the Patapsco, and the Lieutenant of the Cutter was left in charge to bring her under the guns of Fort McHenry, as soon as the winds favored. The next morning after that . . . the Buenos Ayrean Brig *Puerrydon* came down the river and passing near the *Hornet,* the officers and crew

of the latter gave three cheers, which being answered from the Brig, 1st Lieutenant of the *Hornet,* in defiance of the orders and remonstrances of Lieutenant Marshall (of the Cutter) got the schooner under way and proceeded down after the *Puerrydon,* her crew manifesting their cheerful compliance with orders of the Lieutenant by answering them with three cheers. As they proceeded to sea, Lt. Marshall attempted to speak a vessel, but was seized and carried below. Finally the pirates released him at the Capes."

When word of Lt. Marshall's abduction reached customs officials at Norfolk, Virginia, a search was organized for the *Hornet,* but the pirate ship managed to escape.

Two of the Revenue Marine's cutters, the *Louisiana* and the *Alabama,* were especially active in the campaign against the pirates. They were new ships, patterned after the speedy Baltimore clippers with a high stern and low bow. Both vessels were commissioned in 1819 and assigned to the Gulf of Mexico where one of their conquests was the notorious Jean La Farge, commander of the pirate ship *Bravo.* La Farge, in the *Bravo,* was escorting two captured vessels when he encountered the Revenue Marine cutters. The *Bravo,* defiantly flying a black flag, attempted to fight off the cutters, but their combined gunfire was too much for the pirates who fled belowdecks where they were captured by the Revenue Marine men who boarded the ship. The men of the *Louisiana* and *Alabama* also rescued La Farge's two prizes with their cargoes of goods and passengers.

If the *Bravo* had managed to escape, she might have taken her prisoners and booty to Patterson's Town, the pirate stronghold on Breton Island near the mouth of the Mississippi River. Patterson's Town became the next objective of the *Louisiana* and the *Alabama.* The two cutters took the town by surprise and the Revenue Marine men who stormed ashore to destroy buildings and round up the town's inhabitants scored a significant success in the campaign against the pirates.

In a letter written while the *Louisiana* was in the Caribbean her captain, John Lewis, told of further action against the pirates. "I have succeeded in taking four more Pirates which I have now in confinement on board this vessel," he wrote. "I have about $4,000 worth of dry goods which they have robbed and were endeavoring to smuggle into the United States."

Slave ships proved to be more illusive than pirate vessels. The importation of slaves had been illegal since 1808, but the practice continued. A few slavers came directly from Africa with their contraband cargo, but most of them sailed to the United States from Cuba. Although cutter crews managed to intercept some of the vessels and rescue their hapless occupants, others managed to slip into southern harbors undetected.

Not all of the Revenue Marine's attention was directed to southern waters. During the winter of 1831 Secretary of the Treasury Louis McLane assigned a new duty to the cutters. In a letter to the collector of customs at Wilmington, Delaware, the cutter *Gallatin*'s home port, the Secretary wrote, "In the present inclement season it is thought proper to combine with the ordinary duties of the Cutters that of assisting vessels found on the Coast in distress,

While serving as Secretary of the Treasury in Andrew Jackson's cabinet, Louis McLane directed Revenue Service cutters to aid vessels in distress, an activity that was to become a primary duty of the United States Coast Guard. One of the Revenue Service's first steamers was named for McLane. This portrait hangs in the Treasury Building in Washington, D.C.

and of ministering to the wants of their crews."

The *Gallatin* sailed between Cape May, New Jersey, and Hog Island, Virginia, looking for ships in need of help, and her sister cutters patrolled areas within range of their home stations. They were equipped to supply provisions at cost to ships whose stores had run out and to rescue vessels caught in winter storms.

Treasury records provide no information on the number of ships aided by the early Coast Guardsmen, and their humanitarian service may have been discontinued after the first winter because in 1832 several ships of the cutter fleet had to be sent to Charleston, South Carolina. Winter cruising was reinstated in 1837, this time, however, authorized by an act of Congress.

In 1832 South Carolina, in an Ordinance of Nullification, declared that the tariff acts passed by Congress in 1828 and 1832 did not apply in the ports of that state. President Andrew Jackson responded with a statement that the laws of the United States must be obeyed, and the Secretary of the Treasury instructed the customs collector at Charleston to employ his revenue cutter to collect duties from incoming vessels, using force if necessary.

Five cutters received orders to sail for Charleston where they reported to the customs collector. Acting under orders from the collector, officers from the cutters boarded incoming ships carrying taxable goods and directed them to Fort Moultrie. There they supervised the unloading of cargoes which were held at the fort until money due the federal government was paid. The cutters remained at Charleston until the spring of 1833 when the difficulties with South Carolina were solved by the passage of the Compromise Tariff Act.

Revenue cutters sailed south again in 1836, this time to cooperate with the Navy and the Army in the war with the Seminoles who were resisting attempts to move them to lands west of the Mississippi River. Acting under orders from the Navy Department, the *Dallas*, *Washington*, *Jefferson*, *Dexter*, *Madison*, *Campbell*, *Jackson*, and *Van Buren* patrolled Florida's coasts and its numerous inlets and keys. Cutter crews carried dispatches, transported troops and supplies, and blockaded rivers. When men from the *Washington* went ashore to help reinforce the garrison at Fort Brook, they were part of the first amphibious landing by combined forces in United States history, and cuttermen served in other landing parties that defended Florida's settlements. But for the most part they operated on Florida's waters, not her soil.

On one occasion the crew of the cutter *Jefferson* was asked to locate the missing brig *Alney*. After a nighttime search in Biscayne Bay that left the cutter aground in mud, the Revenue Service men took to the *Jefferson's* boats and continued the hunt for the *Alney*. They found the vessel aground and in the hands of the Seminoles. Gunfire from the *Jefferson's* boats drove the Indians away from the brig. The cuttermen then recovered some of the *Alney's* supplies and gathered up equipment left behind by the Indians. The badly damaged *Alney* had to be burned, but the cuttermen were able to refloat their own vessel.

On several occasions Revenue Service cutters picked up refugees whose homes had been destroyed. Often the presence of a cutter offshore was enough to keep the Indians from attacking a settlement. One of the officers under whom the cutters operated wrote: "Their prompt and helpful co-operation with the Army has called forth the highest commendation from commanding generals, who take occasion to eulogize the services rendered by the cutters." And the federal government expressed its appreciation to the men who took part in the war against the Seminoles by granting each of them a quarter section of land.

During the Seminole War men of the Revenue Service transported soldiers and marines on Florida's many waterways.

Men and Ships in a Changing Revenue Cutter Service

Before 1844 there were no annual reports to describe officially the activities of the organization that was to become the United States Coast Guard. While some information about the Revenue Service's cutters has survived, relatively little is known about the men who served on them. However, in 1799 their original ranks and ratings were officially replaced by the designations of captain, first, second, and third lieutenants, warrant officer, and seaman. The officers' titles were the equivalent of the Navy's lieutenant commander, lieutenant, lieutenant junior grade, and ensign.

As they patrolled the Atlantic and Gulf coasts, officers of the customs probably dressed much as naval officers did. An unofficial account records that in 1819 Revenue Service lieutenants wore a blue, double-breasted, swallow-tailed coat with a rolled collar. The description continues: "A button on each corner of the collar, and six on each lapel with four in the skirts. Epaulettes worn on either shoulder according to rank. Buttons stamped with the armorial bearings of the United States, said to be the same

style of buttons as worn by the staff officers of the Army."

Captains wore epaulettes on both shoulders. If an officer was a first lieutenant, he wore one epaulette on his right shoulder; a second lieutenant wore his on the left shoulder and third lieutenants wore none at all.

In 1830 the Treasury Department ordered its cutter captains to wear stovepipe hats, "ornamented on the left side with a black cockade with brass buttons in the center."

Between 1826 and 1832, when a small peacetime Navy offered few opportunities for advancement, furloughed naval officers were allowed to accept commissions in the Revenue Cutter Service. They no doubt continued to wear naval uniforms while on cutter duty. The presence of naval officers in the Revenue Service caused friction, partly because they reduced the promotion chances of regular Revenue Service men. Transfers from the Navy were discontinued in 1832 when Secretary of the Treasury McLane decided that the two services

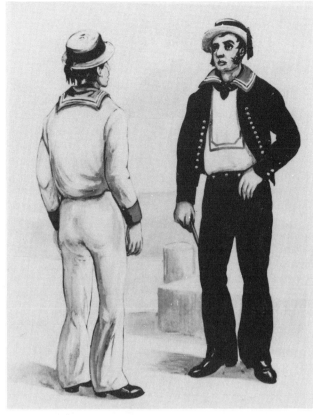

An artist's conception of how American seamen dressed in 1830.

THE AMERICAN TAR.
DON'T GIVE UP THE SHIP

This lithograph by Nathaniel Currier shows how American seamen dressed in 1845, on the eve of the Mexican War.

This illustration of the uniforms worn by United States Navy officers in 1830 was based on Navy orders and contemporary engravings. Revenue Service officers probably wore similar uniforms.

should be kept "separate and distinct." The Secretary wanted vacancies in the Revenue Service to be filled by the promotion of the best qualifed among his own officers, a policy that helped improve the morale of cuttermen.

After a brief period during which they abandoned blue uniforms because they too closely resembled those worn by the Navy and adopted a more distinctive dark gray, cuttermen returned to blue at the time of the Seminole War. With their blue uniforms officers wore a buff vest, short boots, cocked hat, and a small sword on a black leather belt. Buttons were decorated with the Treasury shield surmounted by a fouled anchor. Seamen wore blue jackets with white collars and white or blue trousers and blue belts.

The administration of the Revenue Cutter Service underwent a big change in 1843 when Secretary of the Treasury John C. Spencer established a Revenue Marine Bureau in Washington. Heretofore, the administration of the Service had been largely in the hands of the collectors of customs who designated cruising grounds for the cutters assigned to them, decided when the vessels needed repairs, and hired seamen and boys for cutter crews. In addition, the collectors had the authority to suspend cutter captains for disciplinary reasons. Secretary Spencer centralized control of the Revenue Service in the new Washington bureau and brought one of his best cutter officers, Captain Alexander V. Fraser, to the capital to head it. Fraser was an experienced seaman who had joined the Revenue Cutter Service in 1832 after sailing on merchant ships in the East India trade. His first cutter was the *Alert* on duty in Charleston's harbor during the nullification controversy. Fraser, then a second lieutenant, impounded the cargo of a sugar ship from Havana until customs duties were paid. His rise in the Service was rapid, and when Secretary Spencer needed an experienced officer to head the Revenue Marine Bureau he turned to Fraser.

Secretary Spencer's choice was a good one. Fraser moved quickly to improve cutter administration and the Service's promotion system. And in January, 1844, he issued the Service's first annual report. Under personnel, Captain Fraser listed 20 captains, 20 first lieutenants, 20 second lieutenants, 20 third lieutenants, 45 petty officers, 7 pilots, 30 stewards, 15 cooks, and 323 seamen for a total of 500 officers and men. They were serving on fifteen schooners stationed at Eastport and Portland, Maine; Boston, Massachusetts; Newport, Rhode Island; New London, Connecticut; New York Harbor; Dela-

ware Bay; Baltimore, Maryland; Norfolk, Virginia; Charleston, South Carolina; Savannah, Georgia; Key West, Florida; Mobile, Alabama; New Orleans, Louisiana; and Lake Erie. There were also 149 smaller vessels that ranged in size from two-oared skiffs to half-deck sailboats. The cost of running the Revenue Service in 1843 was $205,854.55.

In addition to reviewing the events of the past year, the chief of the Revenue Marine Bureau looked to the future. More cutters were needed, he reported, and they should have iron hulls and auxiliary steam power. Two such vessels for the revenue fleet were already under construction and contracts had been signed for four more. But additional steamers were needed, Captain Fraser pointed out, because of their speed and their ability to overcome the effects of wind and tide. Moreover, iron hulls required fewer repairs than vessels built of wood, and they were safer.

During 1844 the Revenue Service's first steam cutters, the *Legare* and the *Spencer*, were commissioned, and work progressed on the *Jefferson, McLane, Dallas,* and *Bibb*. The first steamers were not a success, however. Their construction costs exceeded estimates and performance under either steam power or sail was below expectations.

One of the reasons for the failure of the Revenue Service's steamers was the decision to equip the *McLane, Dallas, Spencer,* and *Bibb* with a submerged paddle wheel developed by a Navy lieutenant named Hunter. While side-wheeled steamers had proved fairly successful, the Hunter wheel had not been tried before. It proved to be a very inefficient method of propulsion. One customs officer called it a "deplorable and total failure."

The *Legare* and the *Jefferson*, equipped with Ericson's propellers, were hardly more successful and there were other troubles as well. Iron hulls leaked and quickly became encrusted with barnacles, boilers burned out, and the location of the steam machinery interfered with the sailing quality of the ships.

One after the other, the first steamers, with the exception of a singularly unfortunate vessel named the *Polk*, took to the sea. The *Polk* leaked so badly on launching that she was never used. The others were in constant need of alterations and repairs. In 1846, Captain Fraser, who had advised against the experiments with the Hunter wheels and Ericson propellers, said in his annual report: "The amount which has thus far been expended [$608,158.55 on six iron steamers] would have provided, fully armed, equipped, manned, and provisioned no less than 28 brigs of 250 tons, a fleet which could have formed a cordon from one end of the coast to the other, and a class of vessels which could have kept the sea at all seasons of the year, have rendered efficient service in protecting the revenue, as well as in affording relief, and would have been maintained at an expense comparatively trifling.''

For all their problems, three of the iron-hulled steamers were among the nine Revenue Service cutters that took up battle stations when the United States declared war on Mexico in 1846. In that conflict cutters transported men and supplies, delivered messages, and patrolled coastal waters on the lookout for shipping bound for enemy ports. And for the first time, the cutters went to war as a fleet under the command of an officer of the customs. He was Captain John A. Webster, whose orders directed him to place his fleet at the disposal of the commanding general of the Army and the commodore of the naval forces operating against the Mexicans.

Early in the war one of the sailing cutters, the *Woodbury,* on station in the Gulf of Mexico, was called upon to put down a mutiny on the troopship *Middlesex.* Soldiers on the *Middlesex* were threatening to seize the ship and shoot her captain when a lieutenant, a petty officer, and five men from the *Woodbury* took command of the troubled transport. They remained with the *Middlesex* until she reached port.

The schooner *Forward* and the steamer *McLane* joined a force under Commodore Matthew Calbraith Perry whose objective was the control of the Tabasco River. The *McLane* had the misfortune to run aground on a bar at the river's mouth, but the *Forward* sailed up the river with Perry. At Tabasco the cutter's guns played a part in the victory over the forces defending the city, and after the battle Perry praised the efforts of the *Forward*'s crew. "I am gratified," he wrote, "to bear witness to the valuable services of the Revenue Schooner *Forward.*"

With the *McLane,* now free of the sandbar, the *Forward* took up blockade duty at the mouth of the Tabasco River. The *McLane* remained there for a year, but the *Forward* was reassigned to other combat duties.

The Mexican conflict wore out several Revenue Service cutters. The *Woodbury* was dismantled when hostilities ended. The *McLane,* never an efficient performer, became a lightship after her machinery was removed. The steamer *Spencer* also became a lightship, and the *Legare,* suffering from boiler trouble, was transferred to the Coast Survey along with the steamers *Walker* and *Bibb* and the sailing cutters *Forward, Ewing,* and *Wolcott.* The loss of these vessels and the disposal by auction of some others left the Revenue Cutter Service with only eight cutters in January, 1849. After the *Jefferson* converted to sail, none of the cutters was a steamer, bringing to an end the Revenue Service's first experiment with steam-powered vessels.

Commodore Perry's task force is shown at the mouth of the Tabasco River in a contemporary lithograph based on a drawing by navy combat artist Lt. H. Walke. The cutters McLANE and FORWARD took part in the successful Tabasco River Expedition.

In this lithograph the Tabasco River Expedition maneuvers around a sharp bend en route to the city of Tabasco.

Before American troops under General Winfield Scott made the successful landing at Vera Cruz depicted in this drawing, Revenue cutters patrolled in the area looking for enemy shipping.

The cutter WALTER FORWARD as she appeared shortly after the Mexican War. During that conflict she assisted in the capture of eleven enemy vessels. The FORWARD ended her government service in 1865 when she was sold.

One of the first side-wheelers built for the Revenue Cutter Service, the WALKER was transferred to the Coast Survey in February, 1848, only a few months after being commissioned. The WALKER's career ended when she was run down and foundered off the New Jersey coast.

Revenue Cutters in the Civil War

For the Revenue Cutter Service the middle years of the nineteenth century were a period of expanding activities that included a new coast to guard and combat duty in the Civil War. The addition of many hundreds of miles of coastline when the United States acquired Oregon and California required a larger cutter fleet, and several new sailing vessels joined the eight cutters that remained in the Service at the end of the Mexican War. A dozen years later the demands of the Civil War produced another increase in the cutter fleet.

Late in 1848 Captain Alexander Fraser, reassigned after five years as the chief of the Revenue Marine Bureau, sailed for California in a new cutter, the *Lawrence.* With time out for repairs, it took the *Lawrence* almost a year to reach San Francisco. During her long voyage around the southern tip of South America, the discovery of gold in California changed San Francisco from a small outpost to an extremely busy port. The newly arrived *Lawrence* was the only agency for enforcing the revenue laws of the United States and maintaining order on the

waterfront and in the crowded harbor, tasks that Fraser undertook with a staff depleted by the loss of men who left the *Lawrence* for better paying jobs in booming San Francisco.

Captain Fraser went on to another assignment at the end of a year, but the *Lawrence* remained on the west coast where she was eventually lost in a storm. Her replacement was the *Marcy.*

Shortly after the *Marcy's* arrival in 1854, one of her officers, a first lieutenant who was evidently not too pleased with his assignment to the west coast, deserted the *Marcy* and sailed home on another vessel. A few months later he had second thoughts, however, and informed the Secretary of the Treasury in a letter that he had "upon due reflection" decided to return to San Francisco and "to duty on the coast." The lieutenant ended his letter with the statement: "If same does not meet with the views of the Department—please consider this my resignation—any communications will reach me at San Francisco, where I shall be ready to return to duty or not as the Department thinks proper."

The Treasury Department's reply may be an indication that the Revenue Cutter Service was having difficulty recruiting officers or, perhaps, that the lieutenant had influential friends in Washington. It stated: "The Department will overlook, in this instance, the offense of quitting your ship without authority."

In 1858 the Revenue Service commissioned its first successful steam cutter, the *Harriet Lane,* a 180-foot-long side-wheeler. In the decade since the Mexican War naval engineers had improved steamship design until they were able to produce the speedy, shallow draft vessel that the Service required. The *Harriet Lane* was destined to spend little time on duty as a revenue cutter, however. Shortly after her shakedown cruise, she joined a naval squadron en route to Paraguay to "show the flag" following an incident during which an American ship was fired upon in Paraguayan waters.

In the spring of 1861 the *Harriet Lane* received another assignment to duty with the navy. The Civil War had begun and the Southern states that had seceded from the Union were appropriating federal property and attacking the military posts that attempted to resist a takeover. In response to President Abraham Lincoln's order that federal installations in the South be held, the *Harriet Lane,* in company with several Navy vessels, sailed south to Charleston. On April 12 they lay off the bar at the entrance to Charleston Harbor while Fort Sumter was under bombardment by Confederate troops. The vessels had arrived too late to save the fort, but the *Harriet Lane* was able to make effective use of her guns

Captain John Faunce of the HARRIET LANE gives the order to fire a shot across the bow of the NASHVILLE in this illustration of the historic encounter off Fort Sumter at the beginning of the Civil War. From a mural by Aldis B. Browne II.

Named for President James Buchanan's niece, the cutter HARRIET LANE cost $140,000 to build. After the Civil War she was changed to a bark-rigged vessel and renamed the ELLIOTT RITCHIE. She sailed the seas until 1884. Etching by C. J. A. Wilson.

Treasury Department
Jan. 29, 1861

Tell Lieut. Caldwell to arrest Capt. Breshwood, assume command of the Cutter and obey the order I gave through you. If Capt. Breshwood after arrest undertake try to interfere with the command of the Cutter, tell Lieut. Caldwell to consider him as a mutineer treat him accordingly. If any one attempts to haul down the American flag, shoot him on the spot. —

John A. Dix
Secretary of the Treasury.

Secretary of the Treasury John A. Dix's message ordering the arrest of Captain Brushwood of the cutter McCLELLAN is reproduced here. The last sentence reads: "If any one attempts to haul down the American flag, shoot him on the spot."

when the steamer *Nashville* tried to enter the harbor without showing her colors. According to the cutter's commander, Captain John Faunce, a shot fired from the *Harriet Lane* across the *Nashville's* bow "had the desired effect." It was the first shot fired from a ship in the Civil War.

Meanwhile, some of the Revenue Service's cutters on duty in Southern waters had been seized by the Confederate States. When Secretary of the Treasury John A. Dix tried to save the vessels stationed in the Gulf of Mexico by directing them to sail north, word came back that Captain Brushwood of the *McClelland* refused to move. Secretary Dix responded with a telegram ordering the *McClelland's* lieutenant to arrest Captain Brushwood. If Brushwood tried to interfere with the operation of the cutter, he was to be treated as a mutineer. "If any one attempts to haul down the American flag, shoot him on the spot," the Secretary ordered. But Dix's telegram never reached its designation and Brushwood turned the *McClelland* over to Louisiana.

Another cutter that fell into Confederate hands was the *Lewis Cass,* stationed at Mobile, Alabama. With the exception of the *Cass's* commander, whose sympathies lay with the South, the cutter's crew successfully returned to Northern territory after a long and dangerous overland journey from Alabama.

To the cutters remaining in the Revenue Service, twenty-eight in all, fell the task of cooperating with the Navy to achieve the Union's objectives at sea. These included stopping shipments intended for the Confederate States, preventing goods, chiefly cotton, from leaving Confederate ports, protecting Union shipping, and assisting in Union military campaigns.

In a contemporary engraving Union ships are shown in pursuit of a Civil War blockade runner. Revenue Service cutters engaged in many such chases.

The yacht HENRIETTA, shown here under sail, was purchased for Civil War blockade duty with the Revenue Cutter Service. For a time the yacht's former owner served aboard her as a first lieutenant.

The Secretary of the Treasury urged his customs collectors and cutter captains to employ "utmost vigilance" as they sought to interdict shipments that would aid the Confederate cause.

More cutters were obviously needed if the Service was to carry out its new responsibilities and perform its regular duties as well. The Treasury Department found some of them by recalling vessels previously considered too old and slow for cutter duty. The venerable steamer *Bibb* was one of these. A few vessels were given to the government by patriotic citizens and others were rented or purchased from private owners. One of the latter was the 225-ton *Miami,* formerly the yacht *Lady le Marchant.* She had an English oak frame, teak planking and copper fastenings, and was purchased for a bargain $25,000.

In May, 1862, President Lincoln, with his Sec-

retary of War, Secretary of the Treasury, and General Viele of the Union Army, boarded the *Miami* at the Navy Yard in Washington and traveled down the Potomac River and Chesapeake Bay to the vicinity of Norfolk, Virginia, then in Confederate hands. The *Miami* landed the President and his party on Confederate soil at a point where troop landings for an attack on Norfolk had been ruled out because of shallow water. Convinced that troops could be landed, the President and his Secretary of War ordered an attack on the city. Norfolk fell the next day.

E. A. Stevens of Hoboken, New Jersey, donated the *Naugatuck,* sometimes called the *Ironsides* or the *E. A. Stevens,* to the federal government. The *Naugatuck* was one of the most unusual vessels ever to be commissioned by the Revenue Cutter Service. She was 110 feet long, ironclad, and semisubmersible.

An artist's conception of one of the most famous naval battles of the Civil War, the encounter between the ironclads MONITOR (foreground) and VIRGINIA (MERRIMACK) in Hampton Roads in 1862. The Revenue Service's NAUGATUCK, also an ironclad, took part in the engagement which ended with the withdrawal of the VIRGINIA.

In fifteen minutes she could take on enough water to sink her almost three feet, thus reducing her target area. The water could be pumped overboard again in eight minutes.

A contemporary of the *Monitor,* the *Naugatuck* was with the latter vessel when she encountered the *Merrimack* (renamed the *Virginia*) in Hampton Roads in 1862 and forced the Confederate ironclad to withdraw. The *Naugatuck* also took part in the bombardment that opened the James River to the Union Fleet.

Because of her shallow draft and submerging qualities, the *Naugatuck* led the flotilla that sailed up the James in an attempt to take the Confederate capital at Richmond. Attacking enemy installations along the way, the Union force was within eight miles of Richmond when two barricades, one of spikes driven into the river bed and the other of sunken ships loaded with stones, blocked the way. The Union vessels were forced to retreat under fire from Confederate shore batteries, the *Naugatuck,* her guns blazing, bringing up the rear. One of the guns became overheated and burst, but the ironclad made good her escape. She remained on active duty until 1890.

Among other Revenue Service cutters to see combat was the *Agassiz.* She was on hand when Union forces took Fort Anderson at New Bern, North Carolina. The *Forward, Brown,* and *Antietam* also served in North Carolina waters. The *Hercules, Jackson, Tiger,* and *Philip Allen* patrolled in Chesapeake Bay on the lookout for ships carrying troops and supplies to Confederate ports. And the cutters continued to carry out as many of their regular duties as the war situation permitted.

For the cutters, the Civil War reached far to the

Alvan A. Fengar, a newly appointed first lieutenant in the Revenue Cutter Service, posed for this photograph in 1862. Fengar later became the first Revenue Service skipper of the famous Arctic cutter BEAR.

Captain Amasa L. Hyde of the Civil War Revenue Cutter Service. His wartime commands included the cutter TIGER, patrolling between Baltimore and New York, and the cutter JEREMIAH S. BLACK, on duty off the New England coast.

In 1862 Captain John Faunce, commander of the HARRIET LANE during the attack on Fort Sumter and later commander of the MIAMI, made these drawings of Revenue Service officers' and engineers' shoulder marks for the Assistant Secretary of the Treasury.

north of the battle lines, as far north as Portland, Maine, where the *Caleb Cushing* was captured by Confederate raiders as she lay at anchor in the harbor. The raiders had already taken several Union vessels before reaching Portland in mid-1863. Disguising their ship as a fisherman, they entered the Portland harbor, planning to destroy two boats under construction and burn the wharves. When the wharves failed to catch fire, the raiders turned their attention to the *Caleb Cushing*. Creeping aboard the cutter at 1:00 A.M., they overwhelmed her surprised crew and towed the *Cushing* from the harbor.

A rescue party, organized by the Portland collectors of customs, overtook the *Cushing* at sea, but in the ensuing fighting, the raiders set fire to the vessel. Her crew was saved, however, and the raiders were captured.

Of all the Revenue Service cutters that took part in the Civil War, none was as active as the *Harriet Lane*. From Fort Sumter she sailed north to take up blockade and convoy duty in Chesapeake Bay. In the summer of 1861 the cutter received orders to proceed south to Hatteras Inlet for an amphibious operation against Fort Hatteras and Fort Clark to be carried out by a combined force of United States Army, Navy,

Captain Faunce also made drawings of Revenue Service officers' and engineers' cap devices.
He suggested that two fouled anchors be added to the captains' device.

This engraving of the burning CALEB CUSHING illustrated a story about the cutter's seizure
by Confederate raiders. It appeared in HARPER'S WEEKLY in 1863.

The vessels of the Great Southern Expedition are shown here as they prepared to leave Hampton Roads for Hatteras Inlet and the attack on the Confederate forts there. The cutter HARRIET LANE is the second vessel from the left in the background.

Union naval action against Fort Hatteras is depicted in this combat drawing. The cutter HARRIET LANE is the third ship from the left.

Marine Corps, and Revenue Service units. For the attack on the two forts, which were used as bases by Confederate blockade runners, the Union command had assembled a fleet of frigates, gunboats, and troop transports carrying about a thousand men.

The Union task force arrived safely at Hatteras Inlet and landed some three hundred men before heavy surf disrupted the operation. The *Harriet Lane* took an active part in rescuing men from swamped landing boats and later joined in the two days of shelling that resulted in a Confederate surrender and an important victory for the North.

Not long after that battle the *Harriet Lane* was permanently transferred to the Navy. She served on the Mississippi River and at New Orleans where she became Admiral David Porter's flagship. In 1863 Southern naval forces captured the veteran gunboat and she flew the Confederate flag until the end of the war.

The *Harriet Lane* did not return to the Revenue Service fleet with the coming of peace in 1865, but that year her sister cutters resumed their regular patrols designed to protect the revenue and safeguard lives and property at sea.

A Confederate vessel (left) has rammed the HARRIET LANE in this artist's conception of the capture of the famous cutter. The HARRIET LANE's captain was killed during the fighting and her crew taken prisoner. The captured cutter became a Confederate blockade runner.

On Patrol to Protect Lives and Property

The conclusion of the Civil War brought a welcome end to combat and blockade duties for the men of the Revenue Cutter Service. They were soon called upon to assume new responsibilities, however, for in 1867 the United States acquired Alaska from Russia. For the Revenue Cutter Service the purchase of Alaska meant many more miles of coastline to patrol and other duties as well. During the early years of United States ownership, Revenue Service cutters, along with a few troops and a collector of customs·at Sitka, represented the government, and the cutters were called upon to supply a variety of legal, medical, and other services to the inhabitants of the vast new territory.

The Lincoln, the first of many Revenue Service cutters to sail for Alaska, left San Francisco in the summer of 1867 carrying government representatives to the taking-over ceremonies. For the Lincoln's crew it promised to be a busy cruising season. The cutter had received orders directing it to "make surveys, investigate suitable points for customs houses, search out probable haunts for smugglers, locate fishing banks, inquire into the physical characteristics and resources of coastal areas, and collect specimens for the Smithsonian Institution."

Other cutters followed the Lincoln to enforce the law, transport government officials, deliver mail and supplies, and continue the exploration of the largely unmapped territory that the United States had purchased for $7,200,000.

During 1884 and 1885 crewmen from the cutter Corwin conducted important investigations of northern Alaska's Kowak and Noatak rivers, reaching the sources of both rivers in 1885. The Kowak was explored mainly by steam launch, but Engineer S. B. McLenegan and Seaman Nelson used a native skin boat to ascend the Noatak. They hoped to chart the river's course and bring back reports on the terrain through which it flowed. The cuttermen quickly discovered that the Noatak was a difficult river to navigate with a strong current and numerous rapids. "The current seemed to increase in strength every mile of our journey," they noted in their log.

Although it was summer, the northern Alaskan

The cutter LINCOLN, shown here at anchor at Victoria, British Columbia, in 1870, carried the official party to Alaska for the formal taking-over ceremonies following the purchase of Alaska from Russia in 1867. After ten years of service with the cutter fleet, the LINCOLN was sold in 1874.

This photograph of the THOMAS CORWIN was taken as the cutter left San Francisco, her home port, for her cruising grounds in Alaskan waters. Commissioned in 1877, the CORWIN made her final Alaskan patrol in 1899 after which she was sold.

weather was cold and the two explorers were frequently wet from heavy rains or from getting into the river to guide their boat through rock-strewn passages. Despite the hardships they encountered, the cuttermen continued their journey to the river's source, which they reached a month after leaving the *Corwin*.

Speeded by a strong current, the downstream journey took only a week. The explorers returned to the *Corwin* with a valuable report on the native tribes and natural resources of the Noatak River region and specimens of rock and vegetation for the Smithsonian Institution. During their absence the *Corwin* had carried out an exploration of her own. She had investigated ice conditions along the northern Alaskan coast, aiding several damaged whaling ships in the course of her voyage.

The *Corwin* and the other Revenue Service cutters that patrolled the waters bordering on Alaska did not confine their assistance to vessels in need of help. They aided the residents of Alaska in many ways. Cutters brought doctors and medicine to the sick and injured and food to the natives when their own supplies ran out. Cutter captains, who served as United States commissioners in Alaska's early days as a territory, held court, performed marriages, and provided other legal services.

In the mid-1890s the Revenue Service organized the cutters that patrolled in the northern Pacific into a Bering Sea Patrol Force. From April until November each year four or five cutters, operating under a force commander, were assigned to patrols in the Bering Sea and in the Aleutian Islands chain.

Of all the stalwart vessels that sailed in the Bering Sea Patrol, the cutter *Bear* is probably the most famous. Launched in 1873 in Scotland, she spent her first ten years as a sealer off Newfoundland. In 1884, having been purchased by the United States Navy, she led the task force that rescued the seven survivors of the Greely Arctic Expedition. Lt. Adolphus W. Greely and twenty-four officers and men of the U.S. Army had gone to northern Greenland in 1881 to establish a station for scientific observations. Relief ships failed to reach the expedition in 1882 and 1883.

When the *Bear* began her long career as a Revenue Service cutter in 1885, she failed to impress the Revenue Service captain assigned to command her. The vessel's draught was 19 feet, "altogether too great to make her an effective cruiser on the shore of the Arctic Ocean," Captain Michael Healy wrote in a letter to the Secretary of the Treasury. The letter continued: "With such a draught, all effectiveness as a cruiser against contraband trade and as an aid to

Captain Michael A. Healy, one of the Revenue Cutter Service's most famous officers and commander of the cutter
BEAR from 1887 until 1895. In an article about Healy, "The
New York Times" said in 1894: "He is the ideal commander of the old school, bluff, prompt, fearless, just. He
knows the Bering Sea, the Straits, and even the Arctic as no
other man knows them."

Hunter Wood, a Coast Guard artist, painted this picture
of the cutter BEAR silhouetted against a massive iceberg.
During her forty-one years on Alaskan patrol, the BEAR
became a symbol of the Coast Guard's readiness to help
men and vessels in distress.

The twenty-four men pictured here made up the BEAR's
crew in 1895.

Officers of the BEAR posed for this group photograph in
1897 or 1898.

In 1890 the BEAR was photographed off the north coast of Alaska as she struggled to free herself and the CORWIN (right) from the Arctic ice. The BEAR was the Revenue Service's first icebreaker.

Natives (left) watch as crewmen hoist a reindeer aboard the BEAR in a picture taken on August 28, 1891. The BEAR was getting ready to sail from Siberia with twelve domesticated deer purchased to introduce reindeer husbandry to Alaska.

It's anchors aweigh for the BEAR (left) as she prepares to leave Point Barrow with her relief expedition and some of the stranded whalers on board in August, 1898.

vessels that might become stranded would be seriously impaired if not totally destroyed." But the *Bear* did turn out to be an effective cutter, not only for routine patrols, but for highly unusual assignments as well, and Captain Healy became one of the many to praise the vessel and her exploits during her forty-one years of Arctic cruising.

In 1891 the *Bear* traveled to Siberia where her crew purchased twelve domesticated reindeer which they took back to Alaska as an experiment. If the deer survived the move, it was hoped that the introduction of deer herds would one day ensure a food supply for the Eskimos of northwestern Alaska whose traditional sources of food were disappearing. The next year the *Bear* brought fifty-three more deer and her crew helped the experiment along by building a corral for the growing herd.

The *Bear's* deer were the first of more than a thousand domesticated reindeer brought to Alaska by the Revenue Cutter Service during the next decade.

In 1901, when a larger variety of deer was needed to improve the Alaskan herds, a young Revenue Service lieutenant named Ellsworth P. Bertholf traveled to Russia to obtain them. After stopping at St. Petersburg to make arrangements with government officials, Bertholf and an interpreter set off on a long overland journey to Siberia. They traveled on the newly completed Trans-Siberian Railway and by sleigh to Ola, a village on the west shore of the Okhotsk Sea where the best deer were to be found. There Bertholf bought five hundred animals, all that were available, for about five dollars each. He also had to purchase moss to feed the deer during the journey to Alaska, hire two Siberian herdsmen to accompany them, and charter a Russian steamer for transportation.

When all the arrangements had been completed, the deer were taken to the steamer in boats and lifted aboard. Only 174 deer survived the rough nine-day voyage to Alaska, but they were a welcome addition to the Eskimo herds.

A few years earlier, Lt. Bertholf, then an officer on the *Bear,* had taken part in another unusual expedition that involved Alaska's reindeer. It began in the fall of 1897 when word reached Seattle that eight whaling vessels with some three hundred crewmen were trapped in the ice near northern Alaska's Point Barrow without enough food to last through the winter. The *Bear,* recently returned from eight months in Alaskan waters, was asked to undertake a rescue operation. In less than three weeks the cutter's crew had prepared for the dangerous winter voyage and the *Bear* started north. Because of the ice, there was no hope of the cutter's reaching Point Barrow. Instead, three volunteers, Lt. Bertholf, Lt. D. H. Jarvis, and Surgeon S. J. Call, left the cutter at Cape Vancouver and, accompanied by a Russian and an Eskimo guide, set off overland with dog teams and sleds loaded with provisions. A missionary and a few Eskimos joined the rescue party, which also included a herd of four hundred reindeer to supply the marooned whalers and the residents of Barrow with food.

After an incredibly difficult 2,000-mile journey that lasted some three and a half months, the rescue party reached Barrow where the townspeople and whalers had resigned themselves to a winter of starvation. Lt. Jarvis wrote in his journal: "It was some time before they could realize we were flesh and blood. . . . All was excitement and relief in camp."

The cuttermen brought more than food to Barrow. They carried orders that said: "If the situation is found, as now anticipated, to be desperate, the officers must take charge in the name of the government and organize the community for mutual support and good order. The provisions must be apportioned and as many reindeer slaughtered for food as necessary to make all hold until August 1898, when the *Bear* should arrive."

While waiting for the *Bear* to work her way north as the ice melted, the cuttermen brought order to Barrow, distributed food, improved living conditions, and settled disputes. They did this so successfully that all but one of the whalers survived the winter. Late in July the *Bear* reached Point Barrow. She sailed south again in mid-August after seeing that all the whaling ships were free of the ice.

For their part in the rescue of the whalers, Congress awarded Jarvis, Call, and Bertholf special gold medals for "heroic service rendered."

Soon after it began Alaskan patrolling, the Revenue Cutter Service undertook the protection of the fur-bearing seals that once abounded in Alaskan waters. The Pribilof Islands, where the largest seal herds gathered, became a federal reservation in 1870, but United States jurisdiction extended only to the islands and the waters around them out to the three-mile limit then in effect. Policing this area did not stop the seal slaughter. The cutters had to extend their patrols to the open seas where diplomacy as well as vigilance was required in dealing with the foreign ships that were involved in seal hunting.

In 1911 an international agreement, signed by the United States, Great Britain, Russia, and Japan, outlawed the taking of seals at sea. As the agency

One of the medical officers that the BEAR carried on its Alaskan patrols takes the temperature of a native child during a stop in the Aleutian Islands.

Court was in session at Point Hope, Alaska, when this photograph was taken. The commanding officer of the cutter BEAR (seated, center) was presiding.

Ice didn't keep the BEAR from delivering the mail to Alaskan outposts. This photograph was taken during a stop at Nome.

Seals on St. Paul (shown here) and the other islands in the Pribilofs have been protected by the Coast Guard and its predecessor, the Revenue Cutter Service, since shortly after the United States purchased Alaska.

A boat from the cutter McCULLOCH (on left) approaches a schooner suspected of illegal sealing in the Bering Sea. Sealing vessels tried to remove any evidence of illegal activity before boarding parties from the Revenue Service's cutters arrived.

assigned to enforce the treaty for the United States, the Revenue Cutter Service's Bering Sea Patrol Force continued to protect the Pribilof seals, watching over them during their annual migrations and during their stay in the Pribilof Islands. Today the men of the Coast Guard watch over the seals as they enforce the Fur Seal Act of 1966.

While some of its vessels were cruising off the west coast of the United States and in Alaskan waters, the Revenue Cutter Service maintained its patrols in other parts of the country. Cutters plied the waters of the Gulf, the Great Lakes, and the navigable rivers and traveled up and down the east coast looking for maritime lawbreakers and vessels in distress. The lawbreakers tried to keep clear of the ubiquitous cutters, but to a vessel in distress, as often happened on the stormy Atlantic, the cutters were a welcome sight.

In 1912 the British liner *Titanic,* on her maiden voyage, struck an iceberg and sank too quickly for other ships to come to her assistance. The loss of 1,517 lives, a major maritime disaster, stirred the countries that used the North Atlantic sea-lanes to action. The United States Navy patrolled the danger zone for the remainder of the 1912 ice season, Revenue Service cutters took over in 1913, and the following year fourteen countries, at a conference held in London, voted to establish an International Ice Patrol. The expenses of the Patrol were to be paid by the nations that benefited from it and the patrolling was to be done by the cutters of the United States Revenue Cutter Service. A similar financial arrangement is in effect today and the United States Coast Guard continues to maintain the Ice Patrol.

During the ice season, roughly between Febru-

The Revenue Cutter Service acquired the THETIS from the Navy in 1899. She did most of her cruising in Alaskan waters where her assignments included transporting reindeer from Siberia and participating in the Bering Sea Patrol. The vessel was decommissioned in 1916.

This photograph was taken when the THETIS was in the North Pacific during the summer of 1912. The seated officers are (left to right): Chief Engineer Billy Myers, Captain Claude S. Cochran, Executive Officer Frederick C. Billard and Navigating Officer James Pine.

Two Revenue cutters (with light hulls) have interrupted their Alaskan patrols to pump out a vessel that sank at Lost Harbor, one of the many services that the cutters provided for the people of Alaska.

Training never stopped for the men of the Bering Sea Patrol. Here, they are drilling at the Revenue Service base at Unalaska in the Aleutians in the early 1900s.

The men shown here on the deck of the cutter UNALGA were rescued from a shipwreck off the Alaskan coast.

Refugees from the 1912 eruption of northern Alaska's Mount Katmai in the Revenue Service's cutter MANNING.

The WOLCOTT, shown here in a painting by Joseph Lee, was one of the cutters that patrolled Alaskan waters during the last quarter of the nineteenth century.

For many years Revenue Service and Coast Guard cutters transported a "Floating Court" to the remote areas of Alaska. Here, the court is in session at Homer, Alaska, with Judge Joseph W. Kehoe (right) presiding.

These Eskimos, arriving in an oomiak for treatment by a Public Health Service dentist assigned to the cutter KLAMATH, were given preliminary examinations in their village.

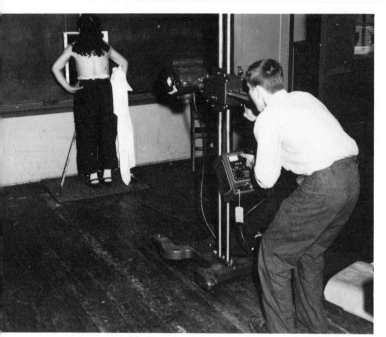

Using a portable X-ray machine from the cutter KLAMATH, a crewman takes a chest X-ray in the schoolhouse at Gambell, St. Lawrence Island, Alaska. The KLAMATH, assigned to the Bering Sea Patrol when this picture was taken in 1955, was assisting the Alaska Department of Health and the Alaska Native Service in caring for the natives of the remote village. Tuberculosis has claimed a heavy toll of Alaskan lives.

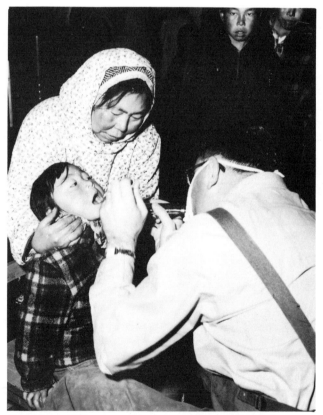

An Eskimo child opens wide for a Public Health Service dentist from the cutter KLAMATH. The examination is taking place in the schoolhouse at Savoonga, St. Lawrence Island.

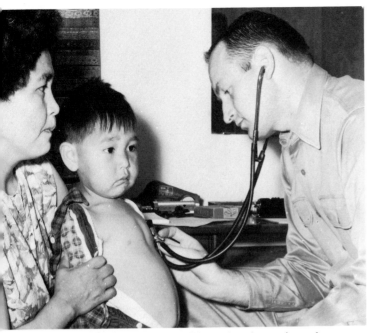

This picture of a Public Health Service doctor from the icebreaker NORTHWIND examining an Eskimo boy was taken during the 1963 Bering Sea Patrol, the last year that doctors and dentists were transported by Coast Guard vessels. After 1963 they traveled by air to Alaska's remote villages.

An Eskimo child climbs up the icebreaker NORTHWIND's Jacob's ladder for a visit aboard during one of the vessel's Alaskan patrols.

On November 1, 1903, the cutter GRANT, based at Port Townsend, Washington, became the first United States vessel to make practical use of radio during antismuggling operations off the West Coast. The GRANT also sailed in the Bering Sea Patrol.

Recreation during an Alaskan patrol can mean a baseball game played on snow. The men are from the icebreaker NORTHWIND. The Coast Guard encourages all forms of athletics on its ships and shore stations.

The luxury liner TITANIC is shown here as she left Southampton, England, on a voyage that ended when she struck an iceberg and sank off Newfoundland.

ary and August, Coast Guard planes and vessels patrol a 45,000-square-mile area of the foggy North Atlantic east and south of Newfoundland where the danger from bergs is the greatest. Specially equipped planes, assisted by a cutter that carries out oceanographic studies, scout the area and the Coast Guard broadcasts the location of bergs to ships. Patrol headquarters are on Governors Island in New York Bay.

Since the International Ice Patrol began, only one vessel has been lost through collision with a berg within the ice patrol perimeter. However, that sinking occurred during World War II when the Ice Patrol had been suspended.

Not all ships that run into trouble do so far from land, and lifesaving operations from shore have an important place in Coast Guard history. The first such operation in the United States began in 1785 when the Massachusetts Humane Society organized a volunteer effort. In 1850 Congress appropriated $10,000 to build government lifeboat stations on the dangerous New Jersey coast, with some of the money to be used for surfboats and other lifesaving equipment. Although the Treasury Department supervised the construction and equipping of the stations, they were manned by volunteers. Paid keepers were hired after 1854, but surfmen did not go on the government payroll until 1871 when Sumner I. Kimball, chief of the Treasury Department's Revenue Marine Division, expanded and improved the existing lifesaving system to form the Lifesaving Service. The Service remained a part of the Revenue Marine Division until 1878; it then became a separate bureau in the Treasury Department. Cutter officers continued to supervise the drilling and inspection of lifesaving stations, however, and in 1915 the Revenue Cutter Service and the Lifesaving Service were merged to form the United States Coast Guard.

Navigational aids—lighthouses, lightships, buoys, fog signals, and radio beacons—are another important

The captain of the first ship to reach the scene of the TITANIC disaster took this photograph of the only iceberg in the vicinity. It may have been the berg that sank the TITANIC.

Rising many feet above the ocean, an iceberg dwarfs the cutter MODOC on Ice Patrol in 1927. Seven-eighths of the huge berg is below the surface.

A rescue at sea. On Easter Sunday, 1914, the British freighter COLUMBIAN, bound for New York, caught fire and blew up in the North Atlantic. One of its lifeboats, located by the cutter SENECA after it had been adrift for ten days, was photographed as the cutter drew alongside. Only four of the lifeboat's original fourteen passengers had survived.

In 1913 the 190-foot cutter MIAMI (shown here) and the cutter SENECA performed the first Ice Patrol for the Revenue Cutter Service.

Named for a tribe of Iroquois Indians, the 204-foot SENECA spent many years as an ice patrol ship and derelict destroyer in the North Atlantic.

Crewmen from the cutter MIAMI (boats left and right) are about to blow up the remains of an abandoned vessel in this photograph taken in the early 1900s.

Because abandoned vessels and other floating debris presented hazards to navigation, Revenue Cutter Service crews had orders to remove them. Here, crewmen on the ONONDAGA load mines to destroy a sunken vessel.

In 1914 when Congress authorized medical aid to the crews of United States fishing vessels, the cutter ANDROS-COGGIN was fitted out as a hospital ship.

The ANDROSCOGGIN's doctor (in overcoat) poses with the crew of a fishing vessel that he has visited at sea.

The cutter ACUSHNET, on International Ice Patrol in 1952, has located a large berg in the North Atlantic.

When she was commissioned in 1921, the cutter TAMPA carried the tallest ship's mast in the world for her Ice Patrol communications antenna. During World War II the TAMPA performed convoy duty in the North Atlantic.

These men from the cutter ACUSHNET are headed for a
closer look at the iceberg in the background. The photograph was taken in 1952.

Since 1946 the International Ice Patrol has been performed
primarily by Coast Guard aircraft. Here, an HC-130-B "Hercules" Ice Patrol plane is collecting data on the size, direction, and speed of a berg. The information will be relayed
to Ice Patrol Headquarters where the location of the berg
will be charted.

Standing in the cargo door of a low-flying ice patrol plane,
a crewman drops a dye bomb on an iceberg to aid in the
berg's future identification and tracking.

The U.S. Lifesaving Service was established in 1871 to prevent tragedies such as the one pictured here. During its first ten years of operation, 14,000 persons were rescued from shipwrecks.

Now a historical museum, the Spermaceti Cove Lifesaving Station at Sandy Hook, New Jersey, was the first such structure to be built with federal funds. It opened in 1849, manned by volunteers who were called out when a ship was reported in trouble.

way that the Coast Guard safeguards shipping. The Coast Guard's administration of these devices did not begin until 1939 although the Lighthouse Service was a part of the Treasury's Revenue Marine Bureau from 1845 until 1852.

Boston was the site of the first lighthouse in America. It was erected in 1716. A loud cannon was installed there in 1719 as a fog signal. By the time of the Revolutionary War several lighthouses had been built on the Atlantic coast and Congress authorized Alexander Hamilton to take over the maintenance of twelve of them in 1789.

For many years Presidents took an active interest in the country's lighthouses. Washington personally approved lighthouse contracts and the salaries of lighthouse keepers. A note signed by Thomas Jefferson reads: "The appointment of William Helms to be keeper of the Lighthouse at Smith's Point is approved. Salary $250." Salaries had increased when President

John Quincy Adams wrote: "Let John Whatten be appointed keeper of the floating lights on Carysfort Reef with a salary of $700 a year."

As waterborne commerce grew, lighthouses were constructed in the Gulf of Mexico and in the Great Lakes, and in 1820 the first United States lightship went on station off Craney Island, Virginia. A system of buoys, begun during colonial times, was expanded, although a uniform marking code was not adopted until 1850.

In 1852 administration of the Lighthouse Service passed from the Revenue Marine Bureau to a Lighthouse Board, also under the Treasury Department, where it remained until it was transferred to the Commerce and Labor Department in 1903. When the Lighthouse Service became part of the Coast Guard in 1939, it maintained a total of 30,156 aids to marine navigation, ranging from 7,976 lights of various kinds to 227 whistle buoys.

This Lifesaving Service station is typical of the stations built during the 1870s and 1880s when the Service was expanding its operations to include the Pacific and Gulf coasts and the Great Lakes.

By the turn of the century, Lifesaving Service stations were large enough to provide living accommodations for the professional crews that had replaced the earlier volunteers.

Sumner I. Kimball, the first General Superintendent of the Lifesaving Service, a position he held from 1878 until 1915 when the Lifesaving and the Revenue Cutter Services were combined to form the U.S. Coast Guard.

When this Lifesaving Service station crew posed for a group photograph in the early 1900s, there were 300 such crews in the Service.

Men from the nearby Kill Devil Lifesaving Station were on hand in 1903 when Orville Wright made the first powered flight at Kitty Hawk, North Carolina, and one of them took pictures of the historic event. Earlier, the station men had helped haul lumber for the Wright brothers' camp and they delivered the Wrights' mail.

After 1880 Lifesaving Service crews used horses to pull lifeboats to and from the water. The horses were eventually replaced by trailers and tractors.

Taken in 1921, this photograph shows the post-World War I uniform of Lifesaving Service crews.

This is one of the Lifesaving Service's first powered lifeboats. By 1913 the Service had 130 powered boats and they revolutionized rescue work.

Before the development of the motorboat, Lifesaving crewmen had to row out to vessels in need of help, usually through rough water. Fishermen were often hired for crew positions because of their experience in handling boats in bad weather.

This photograph was taken during a training exercise at the Rye Beach, New Hampshire, Lifesaving Station. The men are wearing the cork-type lifebelt in use before World War I.

The Lifesaving crew shown here is bringing five persons ashore from a shipwreck. Between 1871 and 1941 there were 203,609 such rescues.

A turn of the century Lifesaving Station crew moves breeches buoy equipment to the water's edge. The breeches buoy, a cork life ring with canvas breeches attached, is used to rescue persons from a stranded vessel through the use of lines extending from the vessel to another ship or to the shore.

Lifesaving crewmen with a line-throwing gun. The device was perfected by Army Lieutenant D. A. Lyle for whom it was named.

Another early version of the Lyle gun.

Introduced in 1848, the life car (above) was a small water-tight boat holding four to six persons that the Lifesaving Service sometimes used instead of the breeches buoy. Like the breeches buoy, it was hauled to and from stranded vessels by means of lines.

Coast Guardsmen from a rescue station in Virginia used a breeches buoy to remove thirteen crew members from a freighter (at right) driven aground during a hurricane in 1944.

In this photo a crewman from a freighter grounded during a storm off the New Jersey coast can be seen dangling in a breeches buoy (at left) while Coast Guardsmen pull him to shore.

Lighthouses and other aids to navigation help prevent shipwrecks such as this one that washed ashore on the Rhode Island coast in 1896.

One of the Coast Guard's breeches buoys in operation.

An engraving by William Burgis that dates from about 1729 shows the original Boston Light with a British sloop in the foreground. Erected in 1716 on Little Brewster Island in Boston Harbor, Boston Light was the first lighthouse in America. It was damaged by fire in 1751 and blown up by the British during the Revolutionary War.

In 1783 this 75-foot tower replaced the original Boston Light on Little Brewster Island. Boston Light was ceded to the federal government in 1790.

Boston Light as it looks today. The bands around the tower were added in 1809 when cracks appeared in the walls. Boston Light became a National Historic Landmark in 1964.

Sandy Hook Light, on the New Jersey side of Lower New York Bay, as it appeared in 1925. Sandy Hook was originally built by the British in 1764. One of George Washington's first acts as President of the United States was to direct that the light be kept burning permanently.

By 1912 when this picture was taken of the Cape Henlopen Lighthouse and keeper's residence, serious beach erosion had made it necessary to move the beacon to the Delaware Breakwater.

Partly financed by a lottery, Cape Henlopen Lighthouse, on the Delaware coast, was completed in 1767. The light was burned down by the British in 1777 and repaired in 1784. This drawing was made in 1820.

This is all that remained of the old Cape Henlopen Lighthouse after a severe northeast storm in 1926.

Scituate Light on Massachusetts Bay is another of America's historic lighthouses. Legend has it that during the War of 1812 the keeper's two daughters frightened off a British landing party by playing martial music on a fife and drum.

The Cape Henry Light (foreground), which dates from 1791, was the first lighthouse erected by the new United States government. It still stands at the entrance to Chesapeake Bay although its functions were taken over in 1881 by the black and white tower behind it.

Encroaching water forced the abandonment of this lighthouse in 1936. Located at Cape Hatteras, North Carolina, it was the second lighthouse to mark the dangerous Diamond Shoals. A new light was installed in a steel tower.

The original Cape Florida Lighthouse on Key Biscayne Bay was set afire by Indians during the Seminole War, forcing the keeper and his assistant to seek refuge on the lantern platform. The keeper was rescued two days later, but the assistant died. This tower replaced the original in 1846 and remained in service until 1878.

Smith's Point Light at the mouth of the Potomac River as it appeared in 1885. The structure was carried away by ice in 1895.

Farallon Lighthouse, 25 miles from San Francisco, was four years old when this drawing was made in 1859. Stone for its construction was quarried on the site. For many years a mule carried lighthouse supplies up Farallon Island's steep slopes.

When the original Cape Sarichef Lighthouse on Alaska's Unimak Island began operation in 1903, it was the only manned lighthouse on the Bering Sea. Its civilian keepers received one year's leave every four years. Families were not allowed because the lighthouse was too isolated.

One of the world's most famous wave-swept towers, St. George's Reef Lighthouse was completed in 1891 after ten years of construction. Located off Crescent City, California, its light can be seen for 18 miles. Waves have reached as high as the tower platform.

Cape Spencer Lighthouse marks the northern entrance from the Pacific Ocean to the inside passage of south-eastern Alaska, a route used by ships because it is less stormy than the outside passage. The lighthouse, commissioned in 1925, is 150 miles from the nearest town of any size. The Cape Spencer radio beacon was the first in Alaska.

Oak Island Light, on Oak Island, North Carolina, is a silo-type lighthouse. The 155-foot-high tower was completed in 1958.

When it began operation in 1962, the Charleston Light Station's 28-million candlepower light was the most powerful in the Western Hemisphere. The first light at Charleston, South Carolina, erected in 1767, was destroyed during the Civil War. The ocean gradually encroached on a second tower, making its replacement necessary.

Passage Island Lighthouse in Lake Superior is located on one of the most important traffic lanes in the Great Lakes.

A new era of navigational aids began for New York Harbor in 1967 when the Ambrose Offshore Light Tower replaced the Ambrose Lightship, shown here departing the station. Lightships had marked the entrance to the harbor since 1823. The Coast Guard has replaced most of its lightships with offshore towers and navigational buoys.

"2 Alpha," which began operating in 1970, is an example of the navigational buoy that the Coast Guard is now using to guide shipping. "2 Alpha" also gathers and transmits environmental data. It is powered by a diesel engine and controlled and monitored by shore-based UHF radio.

Inspecting and servicing navigational aids is an important Coast Guard duty. Here, Coast Guardsmen work on a lighted daymark at Miami, Florida.

The Coast Guard Takes Over

In 1898 the Revenue Cutter Service was once again called upon to cooperate with the Navy when years of Cuban rebellion against Spanish rule culminated in a war between Spain and the United States. Because the conflict involved action on two oceans, the Navy badly needed the 124 line officers, 74 engineering officers, 900 enlisted men, and 19 cutters that the Cutter Service carried on its rolls. Moreover, thanks to three years of intensive patrolling in the Straits of Florida and adjacent waters, cuttermen had acquired some firsthand experience with the Cuban situation.

The Revenue Cutter Service's prewar patrols, performed by six cutters, were aimed at preventing the movement of arms and Cuban revolutionaries from Florida to Cuba, something the United States was required to do by international law. The vigilant cuttermen seized seven ships at sea, detained thirteen others in port, and broke up two illegal expeditions. After the declaration of war, some cutters continued to patrol the coasts of the United States, now on the lookout for Spanish raiders, and one cutter, the Mc-

Lane, was assigned to guard an important Navy communications channel, a cable running from Key West to the mainland.

Word that the battle ship *Maine* had been sunk in Havana Harbor and that war was inevitable reached the cutter *McCulloch* at Malta. The newly completed vessel was on a shakedown cruise scheduled to end at San Francisco, her home port, after stops in the Mediterranean and the Orient. When the *McCulloch* reached Singapore, however, she was ordered to join Commodore George Dewey's Asiatic Squadron, then at Hong Kong. During their short stay at Hong Kong, the *McCulloch*'s crew covered her white hull with gray paint, installed additional guns, and loaded ammunition and provisions. They continued their preparations for combat while the cutter was en route to the Philippine Islands at the head of one of the two columns that made up Dewey's task force.

Commodore Dewey's destination was Manila Bay, which he entered after his ships, the *McCulloch* among them, silenced a Spanish shore battery. During the battle in Manila Bay, which began with the com-

The 1,440-ton cutter McCULLOCH is shown here in the rigging she carried during the Spanish-American War. The cutter then had a crew of approximately eight officers and ninety-five men.

This photograph was taken in 1917 as the McCULLOCH was sinking after a collision off the California coast.

With most of her rigging removed after her conversion to steam power, the McCULLOCH looked like this during her last years when she was assigned to the Bering Sea Patrol.

modore's famous order: "You may fire when you are ready, Gridley," the *McCulloch* watched over two supply ships. In addition, her crew was on the alert for surprise attacks and ready to tow any damaged ships to safety. Her towing services were not needed, however. At Manila Bay, Dewey won a decisive victory without taking any losses himself. Four days later the *McCulloch* sailed for Hong Kong with the news that the Spanish fleet had been destroyed.

Meanwhile, on the other side of the globe, cutters were convoying troop and supply ships, patrolling the Atlantic and Gulf coasts on the lookout for the Spanish Atlantic Fleet and standing watch on the blockade that had been established off Havana and Cuba's north coast.

One of the Revenue Service vessels assigned to blockade duty was the 96-foot harbor cutter *Hudson*. On her patrols the *Hudson* carried a supply of arms and ammunition for distribution to anti-Spanish groups operating in the vicinity of Cuba's Cárdenas Bay. There were three Spanish gunboats in the bay, however, and they made it difficult for the *Hudson's* crew to contact the rebel bands.

In her attempt to clear the bay, the *Hudson* had the assistance of two Navy gunboats and a torpedo boat. The raiding vessels located the Spanish gun-

An artist's conception of the Battle of Manila shows Commodore Dewey's fleet exchanging fire with Spanish forces in Manila Bay. The cutter McCULLOCH protected two of Dewey's supply ships during the engagement that ended in a decisive American victory.

The torpedo boat WINSLOW is under tow in this portrayal of the Navy vessel's rescue by the Coast Guard's HUDSON in Cárdenas Bay.

boats, but they also came under fierce attack from shore batteries. "Shells screamed overhead and lashed the water all around," according to one of the officers on the *Hudson*. The torpedo boat *Winslow* received two direct hits and began to drift helplessly toward the shore. Noticing the *Winslow*'s plight, the *Hudson*'s skipper went after the stricken ship. In dangerously shallow water, with shells exploding on all sides, the cutter managed to get a line to the *Winslow* and pull her to safety. Without the assistance that the

Hudson's crew provided at considerable peril to themselves, the *Winslow* would surely have been lost, a fact that President William McKinley recognized when he called the *Hudson*'s action "a deed of special gallantry." The President asked Congress to award medals to the *Hudson*'s crew and Congress complied with his request.

Spain and the United States signed a peace treaty in mid-August, 1898, and with the end of hostilities the Revenue Cutter Service's vessels returned to regu-

Newly commissioned at the time of the Spanish-American War, the 205-foot MANNING served as a model for several cutters built during the early 1900s. She sailed in the Bering Sea Patrol and was assigned to the famous Gibraltar-based Squadron 2 during World War I.

A captain in dress blues

A chief engineer in dress blues

A second lieutenant in dress blues

A second assistant engineer in dress uniform. He wears white trousers, blue coat, and blue hat.

In 1909, when this photograph was taken, Coast Guard officers wore coats similar to those worn by officers of the U.S. Navy. The two silver bars on each side of the standing collar indicate the rank of first lieutenant as do the two stripes on the sleeves. All line officers wore a gold shield above the stripes; engineer officers did not.

lar duties. There was some question about the future of the Service, however. Over the years it had been suggested from time to time that the work of the Revenue Cutter Service could be performed more economically by other government agencies, such as the Navy. Proposals to abolish the Service were heard again after the Spanish-American War, the strongest one coming from the Commission on Economy and Efficiency appointed by President William Howard Taft to uncover unneeded and overlapping federal functions and agencies. The Commission, in the report that it issued in 1911, stated flatly that the Revenue Cutter Service "has not a single duty or function that cannot be performed by some other existing service and be performed by the latter at much smaller expense."

Alexander Hamilton had established the Revenue Cutter Service in 1790 to protect the customs revenue of the new United States government, but smuggling had long since ceased to be a major problem and the Commission felt that the Navy could handle what little smuggling there was. Likewise, the Navy was equipped to assume any military duties that might be assigned to the Revenue Cutter Service in wartime. For the other responsibilities that the Service had acquired over the years—such things as aiding vessels in distress, protecting shipping, and suppressing mutinies—the Commission recommended a marine police force.

According to the Commission, merging the Cutter Service with the Navy would save $1 million a year, and further savings would be realized if the Lifesaving Service were moved from the Treasury Department and combined with the Lighthouse Bureau in the Department of Commerce and Labor.

The Commission's arguments impressed President Taft who sent the report to Congress with a request for authority to carry out the proposed reorganization. Understandably, the commandant of the Revenue Cutter Service was of a different opinion and he had some strong arguments to support his point of view. The commandant, Captain Ellsworth P. Bertholf, who as a Revenue Service lieutenant had purchased deer in Siberia for Alaska's Eskimos and

Ellsworth P. Bertholf, the first Captain Commandant of the U.S. Coast Guard, at his desk in Washington. Bertholf directed the Revenue Cutter Service from 1911 until 1915 and the Coast Guard from its formation in 1915 until 1919.

A captain in dress blues

A chief engineer in dress blues

A second lieutenant in dress blues

A second assistant engineer in dress uniform. He wears white trousers, blue coat, and blue hat.

In 1909, when this photograph was taken, Coast Guard officers wore coats similar to those worn by officers of the U.S. Navy. The two silver bars on each side of the standing collar indicate the rank of first lieutenant as do the two stripes on the sleeves. All line officers wore a gold shield above the stripes; engineer officers did not.

lar duties. There was some question about the future of the Service, however. Over the years it had been suggested from time to time that the work of the Revenue Cutter Service could be performed more economically by other government agencies, such as the Navy. Proposals to abolish the Service were heard again after the Spanish-American War, the strongest one coming from the Commission on Economy and Efficiency appointed by President William Howard Taft to uncover unneeded and overlapping federal functions and agencies. The Commission, in the report that it issued in 1911, stated flatly that the Revenue Cutter Service "has not a single duty or function that cannot be performed by some other existing service and be performed by the latter at much smaller expense."

Alexander Hamilton had established the Revenue Cutter Service in 1790 to protect the customs revenue of the new United States government, but smuggling had long since ceased to be a major problem and the Commission felt that the Navy could handle what little smuggling there was. Likewise, the Navy was equipped to assume any military duties that might be assigned to the Revenue Cutter Service in wartime. For the other responsibilities that the Service had acquired over the years—such things as aiding vessels in distress, protecting shipping, and suppressing mutinies—the Commission recommended a marine police force.

According to the Commission, merging the Cutter Service with the Navy would save $1 million a year, and further savings would be realized if the Lifesaving Service were moved from the Treasury Department and combined with the Lighthouse Bureau in the Department of Commerce and Labor.

The Commission's arguments impressed President Taft who sent the report to Congress with a request for authority to carry out the proposed reorganization. Understandably, the commandant of the Revenue Cutter Service was of a different opinion and he had some strong arguments to support his point of view. The commandant, Captain Ellsworth P. Bertholf, who as a Revenue Service lieutenant had purchased deer in Siberia for Alaska's Eskimos and

Ellsworth P. Bertholf, the first Captain Commandant of the U.S. Coast Guard, at his desk in Washington. Bertholf directed the Revenue Cutter Service from 1911 until 1915 and the Coast Guard from its formation in 1915 until 1919.

First Lieutenant Francis S. Van Boskerck, Jr., poses in the white dress uniform worn in 1902. Van Boskerck wrote the lyrics to the U.S. Coast Guard marching song SEMPER PARATUS.

This photograph of the 200-foot cutter UNALGA, commissioned in 1912, shows an early form of radio antenna stretching between her masts. By 1915 all cruising cutters were equipped with radio.

helped rescue the whalers stranded at Point Barrow, questioned the projected $1 million annual savings if the Revenue Cutter Service were disbanded. If other agencies took over its duties, they would need as many men and as much equipment as the Service used, Bertholf pointed out. Indeed, duplication of effort might result in added costs rather than a saving.

Captain Bertholf's stand had support in the press and in Congress. The Secretary of the Treasury, Franklin MacVeagh, also argued for the continuance of the Revenue Cutter Service. In a letter to the President he wrote of the Service: "Its efficiency and discipline and esprit de corps are at their best today, and the service is at the highest point of its 120 years." Like Bertholf, MacVeagh predicted that assigning Revenue Service responsibilities to other departments would prove to be more expensive. "Nothing could be gained," he told the President.

Secretary MacVeagh advocated closer cooperation between the Revenue Cutter Service and the Lifesaving Service as a means of increasing the efficiency of both, rather than a further separation of the two agencies, and a well-publicized ship fire in April, 1912, bolstered his argument. The burning ship, the S.S. Ontario, was discovered off Long Island by the cutters Mohawk and Acushnet. The cutters shepherded the Ontario toward shore where men from the Ditch Plain Lifesaving Station helped battle the flames. When the Ontario's captain decided that the ship had to be abandoned, the lifesaving crew used breeches buoy equipment to remove some of the sailors and the cutter crews took off the rest in their boats.

The Ontario rescue was still fresh in the public mind when Senator Charles E. Townsend of Michigan introduced a bill entitled "An Act to Create the Coast Guard by Combining Therein the Existing Life-Saving Service and Revenue-Cutter Service." Although the Lifesaving and Revenue Cutter services had strong friends in Congress, it was January, 1915, before the "Act to Create the Coast Guard" passed both Houses. President Woodrow Wilson, who had urged Congress to pass the bill, quickly signed it and the U.S. Coast Guard came into being.

Congress, in the Coast Guard Act, directed the newly formed agency to take over the duties of its two component parts. "All duties now performed by the Revenue-Cutter Service and the Life-Saving Service shall continue to be performed by the Coast Guard," the Act said. And it went on: "All such duties, together with all duties that may hereafter be imposed upon the Coast Guard, shall be administered by the captain commandant, under the direction of the Secretary of the Treasury."

Congress also directed that the Coast Guard was to be a part of the military forces of the United States, and during a war, or at the President's request, it was to operate as part of the Navy.

On January 30, 1915, the U.S. Coast Guard officially came into existence with 4,155 officers and men, 45 cutters of various types and 280 lifeboat stations on its rolls and with Captain Commandant Ellsworth P. Bertholf in command. In preparation, a board of cutter officers and Lifesaving Service district superintendents had worked out the details of the merger of the two services. Another board met with navy officials to make plans for cooperation in time of war, plans that went into effect two years later when the United States declared war on Germany.

For seagoing forces such as the U.S. Navy and Coast Guard, World War I was primarily a battle against the German submarine fleet, a duty for which the Coast Guard's speedy, maneuverable cutters were well suited. Cutters were assigned to Nova Scotia, the Azores, the Caribbean, and to patrol duty in American coastal waters. Six cutters, the Ossipee, Seneca, Yamacraw, Algonquin, Manning, and Tampa, sailed for the British naval base at Gibraltar to form Squadron 2 of Division 6 of the Atlantic Fleet Patrol Forces. Squadron 2's assignment was to convoy Allied vessels through the submarine infested waters between Gibraltar and the British Isles and to track down subs operating in the Mediterranean Sea.

The exploits of the Seneca illustrate the nature of convoy duty during World War I. One night in April, 1918, the cutter and the ships in her charge were approaching Gibraltar when the British naval sloop Cowslip, also engaged in protecting the convoy, was struck by a torpedo. Disregarding warnings from the sinking Cowslip that a submarine remained in the area, the Seneca stopped to help. Her lifeboats picked up eighty-one survivors from the dark Atlantic. Only six of the Cowslip's men were lost.

On another occasion when the Seneca's Gibraltar-bound convoy came under U-boat attack, one of the ships in the convoy, the British collier Wellington, received a disabling hit and her crew abandoned what they thought was a sinking ship. The vessel remained afloat, however, and her captain decided he could make the nearest port. When only a few members of his own crew agreed to go with him, twenty men from the Seneca volunteered to transfer to the Wellington to help to save her. They were nursing the crippled ship toward Brest, France, when they ran into a storm that threatened to send the leaking col-

Commissioned in 1915, the cutter OSSIPEE spent World War I on convoy duty with Gibraltar-based Squadron 2. In 1919 she returned to duty on the Atlantic coast and during World War II, with her hull reinforced, she served as an icebreaker on the Great Lakes.

The 191-foot YAMACRAW is credited with driving off an enemy submarine while on convoy duty during World War I. Commissioned in 1909, the cutter remained with the Coast Guard until 1937.

Although she became part of the Navy's wartime fleet, the cutter MOHAWK remained on the United States east coast during World War I.

lier to the bottom. The *Wellington* managed to launch one lifeboat with eight men before she sank. The remaining men took to makeshift rafts just before the ship went down.

Luckily, the *Wellington*'s distress signals had been picked up by the British destroyer *Warrington*, which arrived in time to rescue twenty-three men. Sixteen others were lost, eleven of them from the *Seneca.*

The British Admiralty expressed its appreciation for the efforts of the *Seneca*'s men in a message that said: "Seldom in the annals of the sea has there been exhibited such self-abnegation, such cool courage, and such unfailing diligence in the face of almost insurmountable difficulties."

Two months before the end of the war the Coast Guard suffered its greatest loss when the cutter *Tampa* disappeared at sea between Gibraltar and England. She was probably the victim of a torpedo. Two unidentifiable bodies and some wreckage were the only traces ever found of the ship that had carried 111 Coast Guardsmen, four members of the U.S. Navy, and sixteen others.

German submarines endangered shipping in all parts of the Atlantic Ocean and Coast Guardsmen stationed on the eastern coast of the United States were

The MOHAWK collided with a British steamer at the entrance to New York Harbor in October, 1917. This photograph shows the cutter abandoned and sinking. She was later raised and sold for $111.

The cutter TAMPA as she appeared at the outbreak of World War I. As the MIAMI, the name she bore until 1916, she performed the first Ice Patrol for the Revenue Cutter Service. In 1918, while on duty with the Atlantic Fleet Patrol Forces, the TAMPA sank off the English coast with the loss of 131 lives, the probable victim of a German submarine.

constantly on the watch for the deadly marauders. When the British tanker *Mirlo* was torpedoed only seven miles off the North Carolina coast, a tower lookout at the Chicamacomico Coast Guard Station saw the resulting explosion and fire. He sounded an alarm to start a rescue effort during which the station's surfboat traveled through burning gasoline to pick up six of the British sailors. In all, thirty-six men were rescued by the Coast Guardsmen.

The Diamond Shoal Lightship anchored off Cape Hatteras, North Carolina, to mark a busy shipping route, was sunk by a German submarine in the summer of 1918. The U-boat originally attacked a merchantman about a mile and a half from the lightship, an attack that was observed by Coast Guardsmen on the lightship who sent out a wireless message warning other vessels of the submarine's presence. The lightship became the sub's next target. It received three damaging hits before the attacker turned its attention to still another vessel. The submarine returned to finish off the lightship, but in the meantime the twelve men on board had escaped in a lifeboat.

Not all submarines were as bold as the one that sank the Diamond Shoals Lightship. On one occasion, the mere appearance of an unarmed Coast Guard surfboat, answering a call for help off the Massachusetts coast near East Orleans, was enough to frighten away a surfaced U-boat.

For their work during World War I, at home and overseas, Coast Guardsmen received seventy-five awards. They paid a high price, however. The Coast Guard suffered greater losses, in proportion to its strength, than any of the other United States armed forces.

Pictured here is the SENECA as she appeared in the late 1920s when she had returned to peacetime patrol duty on the east coast. The SENECA was one of World War I's outstanding escort vessels.

Keeper John A. Midgett of the Chicamacomico, North Carolina, Coast Guard Station, who directed the rescue effort that saved the lives of thirty-six British seamen when their tanker MIRLO was torpedoed by a German submarine.

In Arlington National Cemetery, a bronze sea gull poised before a stone pyramid honors the crewmen of the SENECA and TAMPA who died during World War I.

New Tasks and New Tools

While World War I raged in Europe, another battle was being fought in the United States between those who wished to make the manufacture, transportation, and sale of alcoholic beverages illegal and those who opposed such a move. The forces favoring prohibition won out. The Eighteenth Amendment to the Constitution, approved by Congress in 1917, was ratified by the necessary thirty-six states and prohibition became the law of the land on January 17, 1920.

The National Prohibition Act placed the enforcement of the Eighteenth Amendment's provisions in the hands of the Treasury's Bureau of Internal Revenue, an arrangement that was to have an important effect on the Coast Guard. Initially, however, the Coast Guard carried on with its regular peacetime duties—safeguarding the customs revenues of the United States against smuggling, protecting life and property at sea, and maintaining military readiness. It was its role as the Treasury Department agency charged with preventing smuggling that involved the Coast Guard in the enforcement of the prohibition amendment.

Smuggling of liquor into the United States began as soon as the amendment was passed, but it was on a small scale at first. In the course of their offshore patrols, Coast Guard cutters seized a number of illegal liquor shipments, but the seizures represented such a small part of Coast Guard activity that the Treasury Department's annual report for the first complete fiscal year after the Eighteenth Amendment went into effect failed to mention them. During the next year smugglers became more numerous and bolder. They established what came to be known as "Rum Row" off the coast of New Jersey, an area where ships drifted or remained at anchor just outside the three-mile territorial limit. Most of the ships were of foreign registry and they were loaded with liquor. Sometimes they moved in to shore at night to make deliveries, but more often small American boats went out to pick up the illicit cargo. Another Rum Row was located off Long Island and a third off Massachusetts.

Coast Guard cutters kept the Rum Rows under surveillance. They could do nothing about a foreign

Crewmen on the cutter ONONDAGA are brushing up on their marksmanship in this photo taken in 1923. Coast Guard vessels were authorized to fire on suspected rumrunners if they refused a request to heave to. However, warning shots were fired before an attempt was made to disable a vessel.

One thousand sacks of liquor, valued at more than $50,000, were confiscated from the notorious rumrunner BABOON (part of deck shown here) after her capture by the Coast Guard in December, 1931.

The World War I Navy destroyer HENLEY bore the designation CG-12 when she served in the Coast Guard from 1924 until 1931. The 742-ton HENLEY was the first of twenty-five destroyers transferred to the Coast Guard between 1924 and 1926 to aid in the enforcement of the prohibition amendment.

vessel suspected of transporting liquor if it remained in international waters, but they could, and did, stop and search the American contact boats. Many of these boats had been built for speed, however, and they frequently outdistanced the cutters.

The growing traffic in illegal liquor was both unexpected and alarming and law enforcement officials were determined to stop it. Among the remedies proposed were extending the territorial limits of the United States, a move that involved lengthy negotiations with other countries; using the U.S. Navy to combat the smugglers, which was ruled out when the Attorney General could find no legal basis for such a step; and providing the Coast Guard with additional vessels and personnel with which to expand its anti-smuggling activities. The last course seemed a promising one and the Coast Guard received nearly $14 million in supplemental appropriations for the fiscal years 1924 and 1925. In addition to fast new boats, the funds were to be used for refitting twenty Navy destroyers mothballed after World War I. Five thousand men had to be recruited to man the new vessels.

Beginning with a treaty with Great Britain in 1924, agreements were reached that extended United States territorial waters to 12 miles from shore, or more exactly, the distance a vessel could travel in one hour. Within this limit, which varied from vessel to vessel, the Coast Guard was authorized to board and search suspected craft. If any violations of United States laws were found, the offending vessels could be seized.

Following the establishment of the 12-mile limit, the foreign rumrunners moved their operations a safe distance out to sea. The Coast Guard then concentrated its attention on keeping the supply ships under surveillance and preventing American boats from making contact with them. When such picketing was successful, the liquor-laden ships could neither make deliveries nor receive the supplies they required to wait until conditions for delivery were more favorable.

The Coast Guard's task was not an easy one. Rumrunning was profitable and it became highly organized. The syndicates in control used the best equipment for their operations, often better equip-

The 293-foot PATTERSON was one of the first of the former Navy destroyers to join the Coast Guard antismuggling fleet in 1924. She was returned to the Navy in 1931.

Outside the 12-mile limit, the 293-foot former Navy destroyer TERRY (right) pickets the suspected rumrunner MISTINGUETTE. Picketing duty wore out many Coast Guard vessels, including the TERRY, which was retired in 1931.

Pictured here proudly displaying her Coast Guard number, the destroyer TRIPPE was described as an "appalling mass of junk" when she was transferred to the Coast Guard from the Navy after being laid up since the end of World War I. Her rehabilitation took a year.

NEW TASKS AND NEW TOOLS 85

During her first months with the Coast Guard's New London-based antismuggling fleet, the former destroyer DOWNES captured the rumrunners EDITH LOUISE, J. DUFFY, K-13645, PETROLLA 10, and WARBUG. The DOWNES is pictured here in port between patrols.

ment than was available to the Coast Guard. In addition to fast contact boats, the rumrunners utilized airplanes and secret communications systems. They also resorted to trickery. On one occasion, a message was received by shore stations that indicated a lightship off the North Carolina coast was in trouble. When Coast Guard vessels in the vicinity were diverted to the lightship, contact boats were able to reach shore with their loads. Sometimes one contact boat was used as a decoy to draw a picketing cutter away from a supply ship. While the cutter was giving chase, other contact boats picked up liquor and made for shore at top speed. Cases of liquor, thrown overboard when a contact boat feared capture, were often attached by lines to partially submerged buoys, to be retrieved later.

In the destroyers obtained from the Navy, the Coast Guard had vessels capable of a great deal of speed although they could not make sharp turns. The destroyer crews utilized their speed to circle a suspected offshore vessel continuously, sometimes training a searchlight on it at night to prevent deliveries to contact boats. But if a destroyer's circle was too wide, the fast contact boats could dash in, load up, and leave again. The rumrunners were also likely to succeed in delivering their cargoes if they could maneuver the destroyers toward shoal water where the larger vessels were in danger of running aground

After a running battle with three Coast Guard patrol boats, the rumrunner NOLA, heavily protected by steel armor plate, was captured in 1931.

The 100-foot AUDREY B., out of Nova Scotia, was carrying 2,800 cases of liquor when she was seized on Christmas Eve, 1930.

This 43-footer, powered by a 100 h.p. engine, is typical of the contact boats that carried illegal liquor to shore from supply ships waiting outside the 12-mile limit.

while the contraband carriers, drawing less water, made their way over the shallow bottom and escaped.

Large sums of money changed hands when liquor was sold on the high seas. Moreover, highjacked liquor was easily disposed of. Both the money and the liquor attracted pirates who became an additional problem for the men of the Coast Guard as they attempted to enforce the provisions of the Eighteenth Amendment. Coast Guardsmen boarded suspected vessels to find them bare of contraband and with crews tied up or vanished. On the 70-ton schooner Victor they found tables set for dinner and food ready

to be eaten, but not one crew member left on board. Another schooner, the Eddie James, anchored off the New Jersey coast, lost her cargo of liquor and $8,000 to five armed men who stormed over the side in the best pirate tradition. One crewman was wounded in this incident, but there were cases where pirates killed a ship's entire crew.

Due to the nature of their activities, rumrunners were reluctant to report instances of piracy. When the steamer Mulhouse was relieved of her cargo off the New Jersey coast, the pirates took three days to transfer thousands of cases of liquor to other vessels. After the pirates had departed, men from nearby rum-

During the years when it was enforcing the Eighteenth Amendment, the Coast Guard was also concerned with the smuggling of narcotics and diamonds and the landing of undesirable aliens. In May, 1929, the destroyer ROE (above) assisted in the apprehension of the captain, the mate, and one of the passengers of the JOHN R. MANTA, charged with conspiracy to smuggle aliens into the United States.

The schooners CONSUELO II and MISTINGUETTE, both with large amounts of liquor aboard, were among the vessels seized by the PORTER during the years the destroyer served as CG-7.

runners released the *Mulhouse*'s imprisoned crew, but no one reported the incident to the Coast Guard.

Although some of those who trafficked in illegal liquor during the fourteen years that the Eighteenth Amendment was in force succeeded in eluding the Coast Guard's patrols, others were less lucky and thousands of vessels were seized with their crews and cargoes. Vessels that were suitable for use by the Coast Guard were often assigned to it after legal action, thus increasing the organization's capability. The *Black Duck*, a famous rumrunner captured off New England, served with distinction as CG-808. The two-masted auxiliary schooner *Consuelo II* was seized by the Coast Guard destroyer *Porter* with a large amount of liquor under two specially constructed concrete floors. She became CG-806. The *Vinces*, another notorious rumrunner, was finally captured in 1927. After a prolonged court case she entered Coast Guard service as CG-821.

Although traffic in illegal liquor was greatest along the heavily populated east coast, the Great Lakes, the Gulf coast and the Pacific coast had their

share of rumrunners. On the Great Lakes, the Coast Guard watched for boats and larger craft bringing liquor from Canada, a relatively short transit. The Bahamas and Cuba supplied most of the illegal liquor that reached the Gulf coast where secluded beaches and inlets provided many places where contraband could be landed undetected.

On the Pacific coast rumrunners traveled routes that ran from British Columbia to Seattle, San Francisco, Los Angeles, and San Diego. The Coast Guard maintained patrols with cutters and smaller craft that often lacked the speed of some of the contraband carriers; nevertheless, they managed to give a good account of themselves. The cutter *Arcata* captured the speedy *Searchlight* after the latter anchored near the Coast Guard craft in a dense fog. On another occasion the *Arcata* apprehended a speedboat that carried both liquor and illegal immigrants.

In 1927 the cutter *Vaughan* employed a ruse to capture the notorious west coast rumrunner *Hakadata* off Mexico's Santo Tomás Point. The slower cutter posed as a Mexican vessel until she had maneu-

Collision with CG-808, formerly the rumrunner BLACK DUCK, and gunfire damaged the speedboat ARTEMIS when the latter was trying to deliver a deckload of liquor. The ARTEMIS managed to get away, but she was located in the shipyard where she had put in for repairs.

The destroyer BEALE was photographed as she patrolled on Rum Row. Cruises on Rum Row usually lasted for several days during which Coast Guardsmen identified suspected vessels, kept them under surveillance, and watched for contact boats.

One of the Coast Guard's 78-foot patrol boats captured the WHISPERING WINDS, whose crew had piled sacks of liquor around the deckhouse for protection. The WHISPERING WINDS became CG-986.

Faced with capture by a Coast Guard vessel, the crew of the rumrunner LINWOOD set her afire to destroy her cargo of liquor.

Rear Admiral Frederick C. Billard, who was Commandant of the U.S. Coast Guard from 1924 until 1932, years during which the enforcement of the Eighteenth Amendment was a major Coast Guard activity.

spite of the efforts of the Coast Guard, smuggled into the country. In one of his reports Coast Guard Commandant Frederick C. Billard wrote: "It is a problem of no mean proportions to guard the 10,000 miles of coast line of the United States, with its inlets, bays, sounds, coves, rivers and other indentations almost without number offering potential hiding places, against the crafty rumrunner who is thoroughly familiar with the shore line." Nevertheless, the Coast Guard did succeed in reducing the flow of liquor into the United States and the experience contributed to its development as a marine law enforcement agency.

The Coast Guard fleet, which had been expanded by prohibition-related duties until it included more than three hundred vessels of 75 feet or larger, was cut back after the repeal of the Eighteenth Amendment and personnel was reduced as well. However, the Coast Guard retained the aircraft that had been pressed into service in the war against the rumrunners. In the years that followed, aviation came to play an increasingly important role in Coast Guard activities.

Although the Coast Guard did not obtain planes of its own until 1926, its interest in aviation began some ten years earlier. In 1915 two young Coast Guard officers, 2d Lieutenant Norman B. Hall and 3d Lieutenant Elmer F. Stone of the cutter *Onondaga*, convinced their commanding officer, Captain B. M. Chiswell, that flying machines would greatly facilitate the Coast Guard's search for derelict vessels and other floating hazards to shipping. Moreover, planes would be very useful in beach patrol and rescue work. The three Coast Guardsmen relayed their ideas to headquarters in Washington. The result was the assignment of Stone and 2d Lieutenant Charles E. Sugden to the Navy's newly established air station at Pensacola, Florida. In 1916 Congress passed legislation authorizing an aviation corps for the Coast Guard, an aviation school and ten air stations. However, Congress failed to provide funds to pay for the program. But sixteen more men were sent to the Navy's Pensacola school and the Coast Guard set up an office for an "Inspector of Aviation."

During World War I, the Coast Guard's aviators served with naval air units and one of them commanded the Naval Air Station at Ille Tudy, France. After the war the flyers returned to a Coast Guard that still hadn't received funds to pay for the ten air stations and the aviation school authorized by Congress in 1916.

In 1919 Lt. Stone was chosen to fly as pilot on the Navy's NC-4, one of the three flying boats that

vered between the *Hakadata* and the shore. Then the *Vaughan* hoisted the Coast Guard ensign and accosted the rumrunner outside Mexico's territorial waters. The *Hakadata* didn't give up easily, however. While boarding preparations were under way, her crew set fire to the vessel. They were picked up by the cuttermen and confined on the *Vaughan*. Volunteers from the *Vaughan* managed to put out the fire before the *Hakadata* exploded; and with the help of another cutter, the *Vaughan* towed her valuable prize to San Pedro, California.

Prohibition came to an end on December 5, 1933. The law had proved to be unpopular and unenforceable. From the beginning, liquor had been manufactured illegally in the United States and, in

Lieutenant Elmer F. Stone (left), one of the Coast Guard's pioneer aviators, and Navy Lieutenant Commander R. A. Lavender. In 1919 Stone participated in the Navy's famous transatlantic flight.

Coast Guard Lieutenant Elmer F. Stone was a pilot on the Curtiss-built biplane, the NC-4, that made the first successful Atlantic crossing. The NC-4 is shown here taxiing during a stop in the Azores en route.

The First Coast Guard Aviation Group posed for this photograph at the Naval Air Station, Pensacola, Florida, where the men received their training.

took off in May on a flight to Europe via Newfoundland and the Azores. The NC-4, the only one of the three planes to complete the journey, was the first airplane to fly the Atlantic. The NC-1 and the NC-3 were both forced down in the Atlantic. Their crews were rescued by passing vessels.

Taking advantage of the enthusiasm for aviation generated by the flight of the NC-4, the Coast Guard, in 1920, set up an air station at Morehead City, North Carolina. Because no funds had been appropriated for Coast Guard aviation, the station was a makeshift affair utilizing six old planes borrowed from the Navy. A tent served as a hangar. For fifteen months the planes participated in offshore searches and made aerial surveys. The Coast Guard hopefully reported that its use of aviation "can now be regarded as an assured proposition," but no funds were forthcoming from Congress and the air station had to be closed.

Four years later, faced with the impossibility of maintaining enough surface patrols to detect the growing number of rumrunners, the Coast Guard borrowed a Vought UO-1 seaplane from the Navy. The plane was based in a tent hangar at Ten Pound Island, near Gloucester, Massachusetts, and from there flew daily patrol flights. The marked decrease in rumrunning in the Gloucester area after the inauguration of the airborne patrol so impressed the members of Congress that the Coast Guard received $152,000 for the purchase of five new planes. The first aircraft constructed especially for the Coast Guard, they went into service in 1926, flying from bases at Cape May, New Jersey, and Ten Pound Island. Although the planes were used primarily to detect illegal liquor shipments, they also searched for missing vessels and, on occasion, for missing aviators. Between 1927 and 1930 Coast Guard aviators flew more than 200,000 miles.

The importance of aviation to Coast Guard operations had now been established and Congress regularly appropriated funds for the purchase of aircraft.

The Loening OL-5 amphibian was the first aircraft purchased especially for Coast Guard use. It had a cruising speed of 75 m.p.h. and a range of 415 miles. No. 1, shown here, was delivered in October, 1926. Three OL-5s were in service at the year's end.

One of the two single-float Vought UO-4 seaplanes delivered to the Coast Guard in 1926 is shown here parked at an air station. The UO-4 was used extensively in apprehending rumrunners.

In 1931 the Coast Guard added five Viking single-engine, biplane flying boats to its inventory: They carried two passengers, cruised at 88 m.p.h., and had a range of 400 miles.

One of the Coast Guard's PJ-1 twin-engine flying boats is shown here after it had landed to pick up a burned seaman. The PJ flying boat, especially designed to transport stretcher cases, went into service in 1932.

Its five-passenger capacity and more than 2,000-mile range made the PH-2 the Coast Guard's "big boat" when it began to fly aerial patrols in 1938.

In 1931 two flying boats and a land biplane joined the Coast Guard air fleet, and five more planes were added in 1932. With the money that was becoming available to it, the Coast Guard was able to obtain planes especially designed to suit its needs. These planes were larger, with a greater cruising range and fitted with the latest radio equipment and instruments for all-weather flying.

In 1934 a reorganization in the Treasury Department further increased the number of planes available to the Coast Guard. Fifteen aircraft that formerly belonged to the Customs Service and six Navy planes were turned over to the Coast Guard when it took over the Treasury's Border Patrol. Many of these planes proved unserviceable, however, and they were eventually replaced.

Coast Guard aviators demonstrated their proficiency in the air when they set three world aviation records in 1935. Elmer Stone, now a commander, flew a Grumman amphibian to a record average speed of 191.734 miles per hour over a 3-kilometer course. Lt. Richard L. Burke averaged 173.945 miles an hour over a 100-kilometer course in an amphibian with a 500-kilogram load and he set an altitude record when

he flew the same plane to 17,877 feet.

In 1937 Secretary of the Treasury Henry Morgenthau, Jr., was able to report that the Coast Guard had flown almost 3 million miles during which its pilots had saved lives, detected smugglers, located obstructions to navigation, aided vessels in distress, and performed other valuable services. "The use of aircraft for Coast Guard duties along the coast and land borders, in flood rescue operations and in cooperation with other Treasury agencies in law enforcement work, comprises a field of great activity and of increasing importance,'" the Secretary wrote.

The Secretary's view of the increasing importance of Coast Guard aviation was borne out. By 1940 the service had fifty aircraft operating from air stations at Salem, Massachusetts; Miami, Florida; St. Petersburg, Florida; Biloxi, Mississippi; San Diego, California; and Port Angeles, Washington, with an additional air patrol detachment at Traverse City, Michigan. The air stations were located where both land and sea planes could cooperate with lifeboat stations. The sites were also selected with national defense in mind, an increasingly significant factor after war broke out in Europe in 1939.

A Coast Guard JRF-3 twin-engine flying boat on anchorage patrol in New York Harbor. The JRF-3, a high-wing monoplane amphibian, came into service in 1939.

The Consolidated PBY-5 Catalina twin-engine flying boat, shown here flying over the San Diego Air Station, was delivered to the Coast Guard in 1941.

Coast Guard student pilots (wearing parachutes) line up in front of their training planes in this 1941 photograph. In the months before the United States entered World War II the Coast Guard stepped up its pilot training to meet the increased demand for aerial patrols in the North Atlantic.

The Coast Guard began helicopter training in 1943 at its air station at Floyd Bennett Field in New York. Some of the early training in shipboard landing and takeoff was from the deck of the U.S.S. COBB on loan from the Navy.

One of the oldest means of helping mariners, the lighthouse, is shown here with one of the newest, the helicopter. The Coast Guard has found helicopters particularly useful in rescue and relief missions.

Coast Guardsmen at War

When the United States declared war on the Axis powers on December 8, 1941, the Coast Guard had been operating as a part of the U.S. Navy for more than a month and World War II had already brought it additional responsibilities. Coast Guardsmen were maintaining the security of American ports. Coast Guard ships and planes were patrolling in the Atlantic to ensure that the neutrality proclaimed by President Franklin D. Roosevelt was not violated. Farther afield, its cutters assigned to the Greenland Patrol were watching for signs of Nazi activity on that strategically located island in the North Atlantic. Cutters also served as mid-Atlantic weather stations, gathering valuable information for the growing number of ships and planes that were crossing the ocean.

Coast Guard patrols at sea and ashore were expanded after the United States became a belligerent. In addition, Coast Guardsmen were assigned to antisubmarine patrol and convoy escort duty in the North Atlantic to protect vital military supplies and, later, troops moving from the United States to Great Britain. Training also got under way for the amphibious land-

ing operations that were to be one of the outstanding contributions of the Coast Guard to the Allied war effort.

In their own vessels and in Navy and Army craft Coast Guardsmen participated in all of the major amphibious operations of World War II. In Europe they carried invasion forces to North Africa, Sicily, Italy, Normandy, and southern France. They transported troops and supplies to Pacific islands from the Solomons to Okinawa, on Japan's doorstep.

The Coast Guard began World War II with its strength at approximately 25,000 men, a number that increased rapidly until it reached a peak of 175,000 regulars and regular reservists in June, 1944. Most of the expansion took place in the latter group—men who were obligated to serve "for the duration." In addition, the Coast Guard recruited 50,000 civilian volunteers for its Temporary Reserve, many of whom served on a part-time basis without pay. The temporary reservists took over shore and coastal duties, thus releasing full-time Coast Guardsmen for combat.

Another reserve group, the Women's Reserve,

known as the SPARS, also took over some of the Coast Guard's shore duties. Beginning in 1943 SPARS replaced male Coast Guardsmen as storekeepers, receptionists, messengers, mail clerks, telephone and teletype operators, radio technicians, clerical workers, and in other onshore specialties. Approximately 11,000 women served as SPARS during World War II.

At sea Coast Guardsmen manned a variety of craft belonging to the Navy and the Army as well as the Service's own cutters. The larger vessels were used to transport troops and cargo over considerable distances. The majority of the Coast Guard–manned craft were smaller combat vessels, however. They included several kinds of landing craft, patrol frigates, destroyer escorts, attack transports, freight and supply vessels, tugs, tankers and corvettes. In addition, some Coast Guardsmen served in the crews of Navy-operated vessels.

ON COMBAT DUTY IN THE NORTH ATLANTIC

During World War II the Coast Guard used sailing vessels manned by temporary reservists for some of its Atlantic patrols. The larger vessels made up the "Corsair Fleet" that worked far offshore. The Walt Disney Studios designed the fleet's emblem.

One of the vessels in the World War II Corsair Fleet, the former Gloucester fishing schooner GERTRUDE L. THEABAUD, as depicted by Coast Guard artist Hunter Wood.

Artist Wood painted this picture of the cutter SEBAGO on patrol duty in the North Atlantic. The SEBAGO was later turned over to the British Navy. During the North African invasion, as the H.M.S. WALNEY, she carried United States antisabotage teams into Oran Harbor where she was sunk.

Known as the Sea Bird or Kingfisher, the Coast Guard's OS2U-3 scout-observation plane was used extensively for antisubmarine patrols during the early years of World War II. Here, a ground crewman checks a Sea Bird between missions.

Thirty-two Coast Guard–manned vessels, sixteen of them Coast Guard cutters, were lost to enemy action during World War II. The 327-foot *Hamilton*, struck by a torpedo off Iceland in 1942, was the largest of the cutters to go down. Most of the 574 Coast Guardsmen listed as killed in action were crew members on the vessels that sank. The Coast Guard lost a total of 1,917 men during its World War II operations.

For their services during World War II, 1,868 Coast Guardsmen were decorated. One of them, Signalman First Class Douglas A. Munro, was posthumously awarded the Congressional Medal of Honor for his part in the rescue of a detachment of marines during the fighting on Guadalcanal.

On January 1, 1946, the Coast Guard returned to the Treasury Department and to its peacetime missions which had continued on a somewhat limited scale throughout the war. By 1947, demobilization had reduced its strength to 18,687 officers and men. The retrenchment was short-lived, however. Recog-

nition of new Coast Guard responsibilities, such as the operation of loran (long-range-aid-to-navigation) stations and weather ships, and the beginning of the Korean conflict in 1950 combined to nearly double the Coast Guard's size during the next few years.

Although the Coast Guard was not transferred to the Navy as in previous war emergencies, the Korean War placed added demands on some of its missions. At home it was responsible for a stepped-up port security program, a responsibility that included ships, harbors, waterfront facilities, and the people who had access to them. In the Pacific, it operated five weather stations, a number of loran stations, and search and rescue units equipped to locate aircraft downed at sea. The units were based at Sangley Point in the Philippines, Guam, Wake Island, Midway Island, and Adak, Alaska.

During the Korean conflict, as in World War II, when its services were needed the Coast Guard lived up to its motto, *Semper Paratus*, Always Ready.

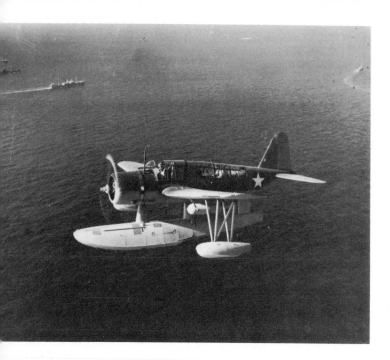

On patrol in the North Atlantic, a Sea Bird circles high over a convoy. The plane carries depth charges under its wings.

Wearing camouflage, one of the Coast Guard's cutters patrols in the Atlantic. The Coast Guard's patrol and escort vessels are credited with helping win the Battle of the Atlantic against the German submarine menace.

Coast Guardsmen, manning a combat cutter, watch over a freighter in the foggy North Atlantic.

Food for the hungry crew of a Norwegian tanker is en route from a Coast Guard–manned escort vessel. The tanker received eleven cases of food over a line fired from a Lyle gun when the sea proved too rough for delivery by boat.

During target practice aboard a Coast Guard combat cutter, a 3-inch gun blows a smoke ring. Frequent gun drills were part of World War II convoy duty.

Vigilance was the watchword for Coast Guardsmen on North Atlantic convoy duty. Here, two crewmen look for signs of lurking enemy submarines.

A suspected submarine was the target when this photograph was taken on a Coast Guard–manned vessel during an Atlantic crossing.

Escort vessels dropped depth charges when echo ranging equipment or a telltale periscope indicated the presence of a submarine. Here, Coast Guardsmen are ready to release two depth charges called "ash cans."

Heavy seas added to the problems of convoy duty throughout the war, but the winter of 1942–43 was especially bad with almost continuous gales. This Coast Guardsman has learned how to keep his feet on a pitching deck.

A Rescue at Sea

Seven crewmen from a destroyed German submarine are clinging to a life raft to the right of the Coast Guard plane that has landed to pick them up. A smoke bomb marks the raft's location and a Navy blimp hovers overhead. Coast Guard Lt. Richard L. Burke received a gold star in lieu of a second Distinguished Flying Cross for this rescue off the U.S. Atlantic coast in 1942.

One of the German seamen rescued by Lt. Burke is being lifted to the pontoon of Burke's Coast Guard amphibian. The seven survivors of the sunken U-boat had been in the water for two days.

Coastal pickets, such as the sailing vessel shown here, were instructed to "observe and report the actions and activities of all hostile submarine, surface and air forces." They operated for the Coast Guard along the 50-fathom line of the Atlantic and Gulf coasts.

The SPENCER Guards Convoy HX-233

A lookout on the cutter SPENCER watches for submarines during an eastbound crossing of the Atlantic in April, 1943. The SPENCER was one of eight vessels escorting fifty-seven-ship convoy HX-233.

Coast Guardsmen on the SPENCER observe the explosion of the depth charge they have fired at a submarine. Earlier, the submarine had torpedoed one of the freighters in convoy HX-233.

The SPENCER's guns go into action after the submarine, damaged by the cutter's depth charges, has surfaced.

With her deck riddled and smoke coming from her conning tower, Nazi U-175 shows the effects of her encounter with the SPENCER.

Coast Guardsmen from the SPENCER (in boat at left) have picked up some of the survivors from the sinking U-175.

A closeup of the mortally wounded U-175. The man standing near the conning tower disappeared a moment after a Coast Guard photographer took this picture.

The last of the U-175 disappears into the Atlantic in this photograph taken from the cutter SPENCER. The U-175 was the second submarine sunk by the SPENCER.

Survivors from the U-175 struggle in the water under the watchful eyes of one of the SPENCER's gunners. The cutter DUANE (upper left) screened the SPENCER during the action against the U-175.

Help! Help! A crewman from the U-175 awaits rescue after the sinking of the submarine.

Two of the forty-one men rescued from the U-175 are hauled aboard the cutter DUANE.

This photograph, taken on the SPENCER, shows the rescued submariners in their quarters.

Gunfire from the U-175 fatally wounded a member of the SPENCER's crew. He was buried at sea.

The battle over, the SPENCER rides in the sunset.

One of the Coast Guard's convoy cutters (foreground) makes a rendezvous with a British destroyer in the North Atlantic. A message has been passed by line from the cutter to the destroyer.

Safety at sea remained a Coast Guard responsibility throughout World War II. Here, a Coast Guard cutter watches over a burning tanker off the eastern coast of the United States.

The CAMPBELL Rams a Sub

The Coast Guard cutter CAMPBELL (background) lies dead in the water after ramming and sinking U-606 in February, 1943. The cutter suffered a large hole in her hull and she had to be towed 800 miles to Newfoundland. This was the CAMPBELL's fifth encounter with a submarine.

Crewman from the damaged CAMPBELL are boarding the Polish destroyer BURZA which also picked up some of the survivors from the U-606. One hundred twenty-five members of the CAMPBELL's crew remained with her while she was under tow to Newfoundland.

A Canadian corvette approaches a Coast Guard cutter in the North Atlantic. Both ships were guarding a convoy. During World War II the Coast Guard manned eight of the highly maneuverable Canadian corvettes.

Coast Guard–manned transports proceed in single file across an apparently peaceful North Atlantic, but the presence of a Coast Guard patrol plane (wing at left) is a reminder of the constant danger from German submarines.

This photograph of a badly damaged German submarine was taken from the Coast Guard–manned destroyer escort JOYCE a few minutes before the submarine, the U-550, sank. The JOYCE picked up twelve survivors.

The Coast Guard's Greenland Patrol

In this photo taken in 1944, the cutter NORTHLAND waits in the ice off the northeast coast of Greenland while her landing force searches for a German weather and radio station. The station was located after it had been hastily evacuated by the Germans.

The NORTHLAND's lookout sighted a Nazi trawler (hull at left) as the cutter was returning from her weather-station search. The trawler's crew had attempted to destroy the vessel, but men from the NORTHLAND (ship in background) found some food and ammunition to examine when they reached the trawler.

Captured in the ice off northeast Greenland by the Coast Guard icebreaker EASTWIND, the German naval transport EXTERNSTEINE is shown here as she approached Boston Harbor as a prize of war. She was taken over by the Navy and renamed the U.S.S. CALLO.

Two Coast Guard cutters leave trails of foam as they circle their convoy in the North Atlantic. In addition to their own vessels, Coast Guardsmen manned escort destroyers, frigates, and corvettes in the antisubmarine fleet.

When this photograph was taken from the Coast Guard cutter in the foreground, a convoy was entering port after a safe crossing of the North Atlantic.

An Arctic Helicopter Rescue

Looking like an insect in the snow, a Coast Guard helicopter has landed in northern Labrador to remove the marooned crews of two Canadian planes. One plane had made a forced landing and the second had crashed during a rescue attempt. The flyers' camp can be seen at upper right. The helicopter was flown to Goose Bay, Labrador, and assembled there for the first Arctic rescue by a rotorcraft.

The Coast Guard helicopter made eleven flights to bring the marooned flyers to a weather station. Here, it lands on a frozen lake near the station. Canvas has been spread to keep the helicopter's floats from sticking to the ice.

This photo was taken as the flyers were breaking camp. During their twelve-day wait for rescue, the eleven men at the camp received supplies by airdrop.

The Last U-Boat

Crewmen on the Coast Guard–manned frigate MOBERLY watch the result of depth charges dropped on the U-853 off Point Judith, Rhode Island. Earlier, the U-853 had sunk an American collier. A combined attack by the MOBERLY and Navy vessel ATHERTON destroyed the U-853 on May 6, 1945, two days before Germany's surrender.

One of the U-853's life rafts was discovered in the submarine's wreckage. Here, two of the MOBERLY's officers hold the raft for the cameraman.

During World War II watchful Coast Guardsmen on antisubmarine duty were responsible for the sinking of eleven submarines and the rescue of 4,000 survivors of torpedoings.

Throughout World War II Coast Guardsmen patrolled the nation's beaches on the lookout for saboteur landings and vessels in distress. The man patrolling this lonely stretch of Atlantic beach was from the Coast Guard Lifeboat Station at Pea Island, North Carolina.

COAST GUARDSMEN ON THE HOME FRONT

By using horses, beach patrols could cover twice as much territory as men on foot. At its peak in September, 1943, the number of horses in Coast Guard service reached 3,222.

Twenty Coast Guard instructors went to China to teach Chinese soldiers how to use horses and dogs for patrol purposes. Lieutenant Commander Clayton Snyder (left foreground), in charge of the training program, poses with his horse patrol students.

The Coast Guard began to use dogs for night patrol work in 1942. Usually a Coast Guardsman and his dog worked together as a team to cover about a mile of beach. Here, the teams are undergoing inspection.

Railroad sidings at the nation's ports were included in the Coast Guard's responsibility for port security. Coast Guardsmen found dogs especially useful when they guarded such areas.

Chinese soldiers and their dogs pose with the Coast Guard instructors (left and right, rear row) who taught them how to use dogs in sentry and patrol work.

SPARs, members of the Coast Guard's Women's Reserve, march during training at Hunter College in New York City in 1943. Women reserves were authorized for the Coast Guard in the fall of 1942 to take over wartime shore duties. The name SPAR derives from the Coast Guard motto, SEMPER PARATUS, and its translation, "Always Ready." The Women's Reserve program was discontinued after World War II and reinstated during the Korean conflict.

A Coast Guard enlisted man in the service dress blue uniform worn during World War II. "P R" stands for "Parachute Rigger."

One of the Coast Guard's SPAR officers poses in service dress blue uniform.

THE WAR IN EUROPE

Two Cutters at Oran

English marine artist C. E. Turner's conception of the attempt by the HARTLAND and the WALNEY to enter the harbor at Oran during the invasion of North Africa. The ships, formerly the U.S. Coast Guard cutters PONTCHARTRAIN and SEBAGO, were transferred to Great Britain under the Lend-Lease Act. They fly the American flag because the landings at Oran were an American operation, although directed by the British. The ships entered the harbor by ramming a boom that blocked the entrance.

Burning and badly damaged by heavy fire from shore batteries and warships in the harbor, the HARTLAND was photographed before she exploded and sank. The WALNEY also sank. The vessels were carring American antisabotage teams.

On to Sicily

With the landings in North Africa successfully completed, Allied forces moved on to Sicily. Here, Coast Guardsmen stand by their guns off the German-held island. Their transport carries invasion troops.

Coast Guardsmen at a North African port load an ambulance onto their Sicily-bound transport.

A second photograph shows the vessel exploding when the fire reached her ammunition supply.

A Coast Guard photographer on one of the transports carrying invasion troops to Sicily took this shot of an American cargo ship burning after an attack by German dive bombers.

On board a troop transport off Sicily, an injured American paratrooper tells Coast Guardsmen about his landing on Sicilian soil.

When peace returned to Sicily in the fall of 1943, Coast Guardsmen assisted in the restoration of the island's fishing industry. Here, a Coast Guard officer talks with a group of fishermen.

Moving Troops and Supplies to Italy

Invasion equipment rolls ashore from an LST (Landing Ship, Tank) at Paestum, twenty miles south of Salerno, the Allies' first objective on the Italian mainland. Coast Guardsmen manned 76 LSTs during World War II.

A closer view of the LST shows its huge doors and the ramp running from the vessel toward the shore.

The Coast Guard–manned transports that moved Allied troops to Italy carried casualties on the return trip. Here, wounded men, including a German prisoner (in peaked cap), are lifted aboard.

Coast Guardsmen with the Invasion Fleet

Infantrymen run down the ramps of a Coast Guard–manned landing craft during one of the practice exercises that preceded the invasion of France. LCI(L)-326 (Landing Craft, Infantry, Large) was one of the many Coast Guard and Coast Guard–manned vessels that carried troops to Normandy on D-day, June 6, 1944, and the days that followed.

Coast Guardsmen are landing British marines on a North African beach in this photograph of preinvasion maneuvers. Such training played an important part in the Allied success on D day.

In the first D-day invasion photo to reach the United States, columns of landing craft move toward France. The camera that made the picture was sold for $8,500,000 in bond purchases in a "Victory Bond" auction.

On a Coast Guard–manned transport carrying invasion troops to France, crewmen prepare a 40 mm. antiaircraft battery for firing. Until beaches were secured and they were able to move closer with safety, transports transferred troops to landing craft some thirteen miles offshore.

Another D-day photo shows a damaged Coast Guard–manned LCI maneuvering alongside a transport to unload her troops and wounded. The LCI later capsized and sank.

This landing craft, set ablaze when German machine gun fire exploded a hand grenade, made it to shore on D day. After the Coast Guard crew extinguished the blaze, the craft returned to her transport for more troops.

On D day Coast Guard–manned LCI-85 limps back to her transport with wounded and dead aboard after hitting a mine en route to Omaha Beach and unloading under enemy fire.

LCI-85's deck shows the punishment she took on D day. The landing craft was able to transfer her wounded and dead to the transport SAMUEL CHASE before capsizing.

Two of the Coast Guard's famous Rescue Flotilla vessels on station with the invasion fleet. The sixty vessels in the flotilla made 1,438 rescues from the English Channel during the Normandy invasion. The fast, 83-foot craft were specially rigged to pick up survivors, and their crews received intensive training in first aid.

Crewmen from a downed Mosquito bomber, located in the English Channel by a Coast Guard rescue craft, are being helped aboard in this photograph.

After giving emergency care to their injured passengers, the Coast Guard crew of a rescue craft is transferring them to a transport (left) for further treatment and evacuation to England.

Six Coast Guard officers supervised the sinking of twenty-three freighters to create a breakwater to protect invasion craft unloading troops and supplies. It is shown here during a severe storm that hit the Normandy beaches shortly after D day.

All Allied vessels served as rescue craft when the need arose. Here, Coast Guardsmen on an amphibious landing craft rescue two survivors from a vessel that struck a mine.

Coast Guard landing barges delivered thousands of men to the invasion beaches. They were loaded from troop transports anchored offshore.

Reinforcements for the Normandy invasion fill the decks of Coast Guard–manned LCI(L)-326.

These troops have left their landing barges and are wading the last few yards to the beach.

LSTs carrying vehicles for the invasion forces followed the troops to France.

Loaded railroad cars moved across the English Channel in Coast Guard–manned LSTs. From the LST's deck, crewmen watch the cars roll away.

Its cargo of war material delivered, an LST fills its deck with wounded soldiers transferred from a Coast Guard–manned assault transport (on right) where they received emergency treatment. The LST took the casualties to England.

Coast Guard Vessels Move to Southern France

The Allies began an invasion of southern France on August 15, 1944. Part of the invasion fleet is shown here with a Coast Guard cutter in the foreground.

An American soldier, an early casualty of the invasion, was moved back to a landing barge for emergency care and transfer to a Coast Guard–manned transport where he could be hospitalized.

Senegalese soldiers, part of the French Army, were brought to the invasion beaches of southern France by Coast Guard–manned transports and landing barges.

Prisoners of War

A Coast Guard–manned transport prepares to load German prisoners for detention in the United States.

Near Toulon, a Coast Guard pharmacist's mate treats a German prisoner.

This photograph was taken on one of the Coast Guard–manned transports carrying German prisoners to the United States.

AMPHIBIOUS OPERATIONS IN THE PACIFIC

The Coast Guard Enters the Pacific War

Aboard an LST in the western Pacific, a Coast Guard gunner is on the alert for an attack by bombers based on the many Japanese-held islands in the area. The Coast Guard's active role in the Pacific war began in August, 1942, with the amphibious assaults on islands in the Solomons group.

Troops enter landing barges from a Coast Guard–manned transport off Bougainville in the Solomons. Coast Guardsmen manned several of the vessels that delivered men and supplies to Bougainville's Empress Augusta Bay while the Allies were securing a beachhead there.

COAST GUARDSMEN AT WAR 141

A foredeck barbershop does a rushing business on a transport carrying U.S. Marines to Bougainville. Coast Guard crew members and marines watch the tonsorial artists.

At Guadalcanal in the Solomons Coast Guardsmen unload supplies from landing craft beached in the shadow of a stranded Japanese ship. U.S. Marines are helping with the unloading.

With a signal flag, a Coast Guardsman on a combat transport calls up a landing craft during an unloading operation at Empress Augusta Bay, Bougainville.

Left behind at Guadalcanal by the Japanese, a two-man submarine was salvaged by Coast Guardsmen who turned it over to naval officers for examination.

Smoke screens were one of the devices used by Coast Guard–manned LSTs to protect vessels in their invasion convoys. This photograph was taken in the southwest Pacific.

A big one that didn't get away. The Coast Guard crew of a troop transport is about to hoist aboard a Navy seaplane that was forced down in the Pacific. Coast Guardsmen in a boat towed the plane to the transport.

The Assault on the Gilberts

This photograph, taken in November, 1943, shows loading operations under way for the invasion of Tarawa in the Gilbert Islands.

Off Tarawa, marines wait on a Coast Guard–manned transport for the landing barges that will take them ashore. Although the scene here is peaceful, the first troops to land met strong enemy resistance. After four days of fighting, Tarawa was secured on November 24.

No. 69 was one of five Coast Guard–manned LSTs that delivered men and equipment during the attack on Tarawa.

On Makin Island, 100 miles north of Tarawa, a Coast Guardsman poses beside a dummy coast artillery gun made from a coconut tree. A number of such "guns" were left behind by the Japanese.

The Coast Guard at Cape Gloucester

This photograph was taken from a Coast Guard–manned LST anchored at Cape Gloucester (foreground) as a Japanese bomb landed between it and a neighboring vessel. Such near misses damaged several ships in the invasion fleet.

Crammed with men and supplies, a Coast Guard–manned LST heads for Cape Gloucester, New Britain, in December, 1943. At the time of the Allied invasion, the Japanese had occupied Cape Gloucester for a year and 10,000 of their troops were believed to be stationed there.

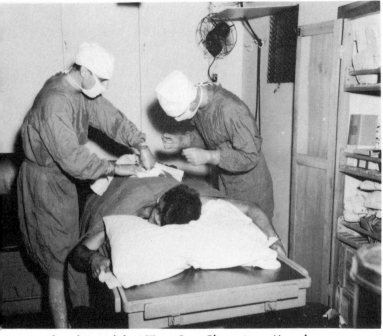

Aboard one of the LSTs at Cape Gloucester, a Navy doctor and a Coast Guard pharmacist's mate perform an emergency operation on a man wounded in a Japanese bombing attack.

Marines pour ashore from Coast Guard– and Navy–manned LSTs in this photograph taken at Cape Gloucester. On the first day of the invasion, 12,500 troops and 7,600 tons of equipment were landed.

Gunners on Coast Guard–manned LST-66 have painted a Japanese flag on their gun turret for each of the three enemy bombers they shot down at Cape Gloucester. Two men on LST-66 were killed and seven were wounded during air raids on the landing forces.

A beached LST awaits unloading at Cape Gloucester. The trees in the background show the effects of the Allied bombing that preceded the landings.

Ready for action, a tank splashes through the water at Cape Gloucester. No. 202 was one of the nine Coast Guard–manned LSTs that took part in the invasion of Cape Gloucester.

In this photograph taken at Cape Gloucester, Coast Guardsmen and marines are combining a cooling dip in the ocean with the unloading of one of the LSTs that brought supplies for the Allied conquest of New Britain Island.

After the Japanese defeat on New Britain, a Coast Guard–manned transport returned battle-weary marines to the Russell Islands for a rest period.

The Landings in the Marshall Islands

En route to the Marshall Islands, a Coast Guard–manned transport (foreground) lays a protective smoke screen. Exclusive of aircraft carriers and submarines, 297 vessels took part in the invasion of the Marshalls that began on January 31, 1944.

When this photograph was taken by a Coast Guardsman, troops had already been landed on Kwajalein Atoll in the Marshalls from the transports anchored in the lagoon. A total of 41,446 troops were put ashore during the invasion operations.

Supplies for the Kwajalein invaders are heaped on the deck of an LST. They have been transferred from the Coast Guard–manned transport in the background.

Landing craft are carrying troops for the invasion of Namur and Roi in the Marshall Islands in this picture taken by a Coast Guard photographer. Two weeks after the landings American planes were using the airfield on Roi.

At Eniwetok, the westernmost island in the Marshalls, the Japanese put up a stubborn defense against the invading Americans. Here, crewmen on a Coast Guard–manned transport assist a marine who has returned from the fighting on the island.

A Coast Guardsman extends a helping hand to a marine wounded during the assault on Eniwetok. Of the 8,000 troops who landed on Eniwetok, 78 were killed, 166 were wounded, and 7 were reported missing in action.

Some Coast Guard–manned vessels in the Pacific carried observation planes. Here, an amphibian is being lowered into the water with two Coast Guardsmen riding its wings to keep the plane balanced.

Supplies for the Eniwetok operation are piled on the beach. The Coast Guard–manned landing craft that delivered them can be seen in the background.

When Coast Guardsmen beached their landing craft on Emirau Island, in the Mathias group, in March, 1944, the natives offered to help unload. The invading marines met no enemy resistance on the tiny island.

Action on New Guinea's North Coast

Headed for the north coast of Dutch New Guinea, a steam shovel lumbers aboard a Coast Guard–manned LST. Coast Guardsmen manned twenty-one of the vessels taking part in the amphibious operations that completed the conquest of the 1,200-mile-long island. Earlier, Allied ground forces had occupied the southern part of New Guinea.

The landing at Aitape, Dutch New Guinea, on April 22, 1944. Taken by surprise, the Japanese at Aitape put up little resistance.

Traffic on Pacific invasion beaches was directed by Coast Guard and Navy signalmen. Here, a Coast Guardsman waves his semaphore flags on the beach at Aitape.

These Americans, disembarking from LSTs in the Wakde Islands off New Guinea on May 17, 1944, met strong enemy opposition, but it ceased after two days.

Coast Guardsmen from the LSTs in the background man a 20 mm. antiaircraft gun on the beach at Biak Island where landings began on May 27, 1944. Although there was little resistance on the beach, the Japanese fought hard farther inland.

Barrels of aviation fuel cover the beach at Biak. The island's three airfields provided valuable forward bases for Allied air forces.

Ready to go, amphibious tanks line up for loading aboard one of the Coast Guard's LSTs bound for Japanese-held Cape Sansapor in New Guinea.

Orderly columns of landing craft approach Cape Sansapor in this photograph taken from a Coast Guard–manned LST. The conquest of Cape Sansapor on July 30, 1944, completed the amphibious sweep along the northern New Guinea coast.

Saipan, Guam, and Tinian, Steps to the Philippines

From a landing barge offshore, a Coast Guard cameraman made this photograph of flak aimed at American bombers over Saipan at the beginning of one of the great amphibious operations of the Pacific War.

The large attack force assembled for the invasion of Saipan crowded the water around that strategic island. The invasion began on the morning of June 15, 1944.

Landing barges, manned by Coast Guardsmen, carry troops from transports to the beaches during the Saipan invasion. Eight thousand troops and nearly 150 light tanks were landed during the first half hour of the operation despite heavy enemy fire.

Three Americans killed during the assault on Saipan are buried at sea from a Coast Guard–manned transport.

Coast Guardsmen on landing craft lying offshore observe the result of a direct hit on a Japanese oil dump during the attack on Saipan.

This photograph was taken during the ceremony at which eighteen Coast Guardsmen received awards for their bravery during the invasion of Saipan. The Coast Guardsmen located a channel through a coral reef to deliver reinforcements and supplies to beleaguered marines who were then able to turn back a strong counterattack.

Some of the landing craft that brought 37,292 marines and 19,423 Army troops to Guam during the invasion that began on July 21, 1944.

Coast Guardsmen help marines unload a war dog (in box) from a landing barge at Guam. Dogs were used to ferret out Japanese hidden on the island.

When wounded men were evacuated, Coast Guardsmen served as litter bearers. Here, with the help of marines, they carry a casualty of the Guam invasion onto a landing craft for transfer to a hospital ship. By November 14, when the last Japanese opposition had been eliminated on Guam, 5,648 Americans had been wounded. American dead numbered 1,289.

Shallow water halted Coast Guard–manned landing craft 100 yards from shore during the invasion of Tinian that began on July 24, 1944. Troops had to wade to the rocky shore of the small island which they secured after nine days of fighting.

Coast Guardsmen and marines break the journey from one Pacific island to another with a swim alongside their troop transport.

Tons of mail followed American troops across the Pacific. Here, Coast Guardsmen survey the mailbags they have just transferred from a transport to a landing barge.

Coast Guardsmen Move on to Morotai

Nineteen Coast Guard–manned vessels took part in the landings on Morotai in the Halhahera Islands. A portion of the invasion fleet is shown here.

The victim of a sniper's bullet is carried to a Coast Guard–manned landing barge during the invasion of Morotai. The landing barge will carry him to a hospital ship.

Some of the 45,000 troops that were landed on Morotai in the two weeks after D day on September 15 wade ashore. They met with little resistance from the Japanese on the island.

The Return to the Philippines

Troops on Coast Guard–manned landing barges watch an air battle overhead as they move toward a beach on Leyte Island in the Philippines. The assault on Leyte, which began on October 20, 1944, was the first major action in the Allied return to the Philippine Islands.

A landing at Leyte's Red Beach, one of the four beaches where the Allies put troops ashore. Four Coast Guardsmen were in the advance beach party at Red Beach.

The Stars and Stripes flies again on Leyte. The Coast Guardsman in the picture came ashore from an LST with a beach party.

Coast Guardsmen on an LST off Leyte watch a hospital ship leave with some of the wounded from the fighting on the island.

Trouble off Mindoro. Heavy Japanese air attacks damaged several Allied vessels during landing operations on Mindoro in the Philippines. Here, an LST has been hit and set afire while smoke pours from a second burning LST.

En route to the invasion of Luzon the Coast Guard–manned transport CALLAWAY (right) was hit by one of the three planes downed by her guns. The resulting blaze was brought under control and the CALLAWAY continued on to Luzon.

Bodies of some of the thirty men killed when the Japanese plane hit the CALLAWAY await burial at sea. An additional twenty men were wounded.

Combat troops climb down the landing nets of a Coast Guard–manned transport into the barges that will take them ashore at the beginning of the Allied invasion of Luzon on January 9, 1945.

Part of the 68,000-man American force landed on Luzon during the first day of the invasion heads for shore in Coast Guard–manned barges.

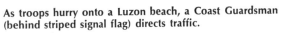

As troops hurry onto a Luzon beach, a Coast Guardsman (behind striped signal flag) directs traffic.

Evacuees from an internment camp in the Philippines, one of several groups of children moved to the United States on Coast Guard–manned transports, listen to a Coast Guardsman play his accordion.

Natives in outrigger canoes greet a Coast Guard–manned transport in the Philippines. They have souvenirs to sell and they dive for coins thrown from the transport.

Stormy weather brings out the Coast Guard crew of a U.S. Army freight ship to cover hatches with tarpaulins. The low-draft supply vessels delivered war equipment to the American forces moving from island to island across the Pacific.

One Coast Guard–manned transport carried a cargo of pennies, nickels, dimes, quarters, and half dollars to the Pacific. This photograph was taken in the transport's hold.

During World War II the Coast Guard established thirty-one loran (long-range navigation) stations in the Pacific. One of them is pictured here. A wartime development, loran is a system of fixing the position of a ship or plane by measuring the difference in the time of reception of two synchronized radio signals. The Coast Guard continues to operate loran stations throughout the world.

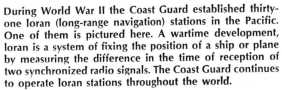

Closing in on Japan at Iwo Jima,
the Keramas, and Okinawa

This photograph was taken from the fantail of a Coast Guard–manned transport, part of a large Allied force en route to Iwo Jima in February, 1945.

A breeches buoy transfers a doctor from one ship to another in an Iwo Jima–bound convoy. The doctor performed an emergency appendectomy.

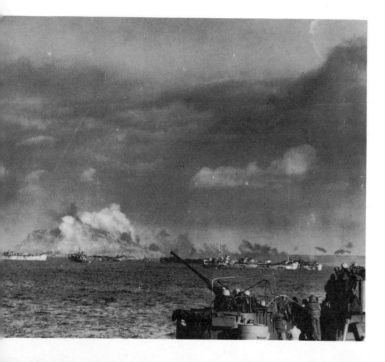

Naval guns bombard heavily fortified Iwo Jima prior to the Allied landings on the island. An LST, one of twenty Coast Guard–manned vessels that took part in the invasion, waits in the foreground.

Amtracks (amphibious tractors) carry other marines from offshore LSTs to IWO's beaches.

Loaded with marines, a DUKW (duck, an amphibious surfboat) leaves LST-782 bound for Iwo Jima where fierce fighting awaited the invaders.

Wounded by a direct hit on an amtrack, a marine is helped onto a landing craft by its Coast Guard crew. He was taken to an LST fitted as a temporary hospital ship. Casualties were heavy on both sides during the assault on Iwo Jima.

On Aka Shima the flag goes up as Coast Guardsmen and troops salute. The landings on Aka Shima and other islands in the Keramas were a preliminary to the invasion of Okinawa, which brought the Allies within 400 miles of the Japanese mainland. In the Keramas a Coast Guard–manned LST landed the first American troops on Japanese colonial soil.

The landings on Iwo Jima, carried out under heavy mortar and artillery fire, were made more difficult by pounding surf. Here, beach parties attempt to salvage two amphibious vehicles.

Coast Guard– and Navy–manned vessels ride quietly at anchor off Okinawa on the day after the invasion of that island. Four days later, however, the Japanese began a series of deadly attacks with suicide ships and planes. Japanese resistance ended on June 21.

The Last Combat Mission

En route from Morotai to Borneo where they will attack Balikpapan, troops of the Seventh Australian Army lounge on the deck of a Coast Guard–manned LST.

Former heavyweight champion boxer Jack Dempsey (right) served as a Coast Guard commander during the invasion of Okinawa. He is shown here with war correspondent Ernie Pyle.

Burning oil fields greeted the Allied invaders when they reached Balikpapan on July 1, 1945. Here, a Coast Guardsman calls instructions to an adjoining landing craft.

Bombed warehouses greet the first Coast Guardsmen to arrive at the Yokosuka naval base near Tokyo after the Japanese surrender on August 14, 1945.

A Coast Guard photographer and an Australian soldier have their picture taken after the Balikpapan landing. The Allies met little enemy opposition on the beach, although the Japanese fought hard farther inland.

For some months after the end of World War II Coast Guardsmen manned vessels that moved occupation forces and supplies to Europe and Japan and returned troops to the United States for demobilization.

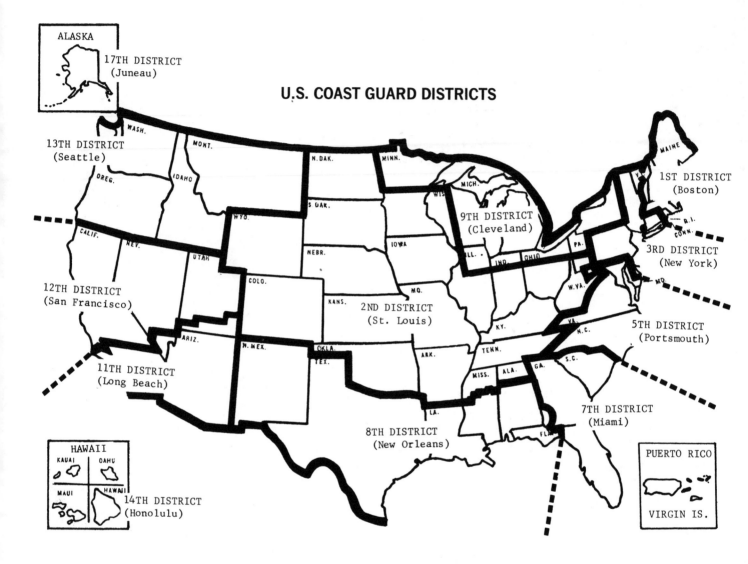

U.S. COAST GUARD DISTRICTS

ALASKA
17TH DISTRICT
(Juneau)

13TH DISTRICT
(Seattle)

1ST DISTRICT
(Boston)

9TH DISTRICT
(Cleveland)

3RD DISTRICT
(New York)

12TH DISTRICT
(San Francisco)

2ND DISTRICT
(St. Louis)

5TH DISTRICT
(Portsmouth)

11TH DISTRICT
(Long Beach)

HAWAII

KAUAI   OAHU

MAUI   HAWAII

14TH DISTRICT
(Honolulu)

8TH DISTRICT
(New Orleans)

7TH DISTRICT
(Miami)

PUERTO RICO

VIRGIN IS.

Serving the Nation in Many Ways

After nearly 177 years in the Treasury Department, the Coast Guard was transferred to the newly created Department of Transportation on April 1, 1967. A federal agency to formulate national transportation policies and encourage the development of transportation systems had been proposed as early as 1805, and Congress considered the idea on several occasions before finally establishing the new department in 1966 to oversee all of the nation's transportation activities.

Because so many of the Coast Guard's peacetime missions involved transportation, it was moved to the Department of Transportation. Other agencies in the department are the Federal Aviation Administration, the Federal Highway Administration, the Federal Railroad Administration, the Urban Mass Transportation Administration, the National Highway Traffic Safety Administration, the St. Lawrence Seaway Development Corporation, and the National Transportation Safety Board.

Within the new department the Coast Guard retained its headquarters organization under the direction of the Commandant of the Coast Guard, a four-star admiral, and its district and area commands. There are twelve Coast Guard districts: the 1st with headquarters at Boston, Massachusetts; the 2nd with headquarters at St. Louis, Missouri (covering all of the western rivers); the 3rd with headquarters at New York; the 5th at Portsmouth, Virginia; the 7th at Miami, Florida; the 8th at New Orleans, Louisiana; the 9th at Cleveland, Ohio (covering the Great Lakes); the 11th at Long Beach, California; the 12th at San Francisco, California; the 13th at Seattle, Washington; the 14th at Honolulu, Hawaii; and the 17th at Juneau, Alaska. The 1st, 3rd, 5th, 7th, and 8th districts make up the Eastern Coast Guard area; the last five are in the Western area. Each area is under the direction of a commander who is responsible for planning, control, and coordination when the facilities of more than one district in his area are required for an operation. The two inland districts, St. Louis and Cleveland, operate directly under the Coast Guard Commandant.

As a component of the Department of Transportation the Coast Guard continues to carry out the missions that were assigned to it during its many

Surrounded by Congressmen and officials from the Treasury Department and the Coast Guard, President Harry S. Truman signs a bill defining the missions of the Coast Guard. The ceremony took place on August 4, 1949, the Coast Guard's 159th anniversary.

The Coast Guardsman on the left wears the new blue uniform; his companion wears the traditional Coast Guard winter dress blues.

years in the Treasury Department. It remains the federal government's seagoing law enforcement agency with responsibilities extending to all waters over which the United States had jurisdiction. Coast Guard officers have the authority to board any vessel subject to United States laws, to examine the vessel's documents, to search the vessel and to use force if necessary to compel compliance with the law. They can make arrests and seize illegal cargoes.

When the Coast Guard was established in 1790, its primary duty was enforcing the customs laws of the new United States government. Although the service has acquired many additional law enforcement duties since then, it still seeks to prevent the illegal landing of dutiable goods. A related law enforcement activity is the detection of attempts to land prohibited imports such as narcotics. This work is done in cooperation with the Bureau of Customs and other government agencies. Coast Guard patrol craft also check American vessels to determine if they are actually engaging in the type of activity for which they have been documented by the Bureau of the Customs.

Another enforcement duty of the Coast Guard involves navigation laws. The Coast Guard ensures that all vessels observe certain rules while operating in United States waters and that American vessels obey international rules while on the high seas.

Through its Captains of the Port the Coast Guard enforces regulations to promote the security and safety of United States ports. Coast Guardsmen assigned to port security forces patrol anchorage areas and supervise the loading and unloading of explosives in the special areas set aside for hazardous cargoes. The Captain of the Port can authorize the search of waterfront facilities and vessels in port if he feels it will contribute to the safety of the port, and he can order the removal of anything or any vessel he considers dangerous.

Because of the importance of marine safety to the war effort, the Bureau of Marine Inspection and Navigation was temporarily transferred to the Coast Guard in 1942. The transfer became permanent in 1946. In their enforcement of marine safety laws, Coast Guard inspectors supervise the building of American merchant ships beginning with the planning stage. They regularly inspect American ships for safety. Foreign ships that carry passengers from American ports must also submit to Coast Guard inspection. Coast Guard shipping commissioners supervise the hiring, discharge, and payment of merchant seamen on vessels on foreign voyages and those traveling between Atlantic and Pacific ports.

When vessels are involved in collisions or other incidents in United States waters, or when American vessels are involved in a reportable accident or casualty anywhere, the Coast Guard investigates. The investigations are undertaken not only to determine responsibility, but also to prevent similar accidents in the future.

Motorboats, by definition, any boat 65 feet or less that is propelled by machinery, also come under Coast Guard supervision because of federal laws governing their use. The large number of motorboats operated on United States waters makes enforcing motorboat laws an important Coast Guard activity. Coast Guardsmen are authorized to check motorboats for such things as lights, signals, and safety equipment. They also enforce special regulations when passengers are carried for hire.

Since the inauguration of the Bering Sea Patrol, the Coast Guard has enforced laws aimed at conserving maritime resources. Coast Guard vessels continue to protect seals in the Bering Sea and, in cooperation with the Fish and Wildlife Service, they enforce conservation agreements that protect halibut, salmon, cod, tanner crab, and king crab. With certain exceptions, foreign vessels are prohibited from fishing within 12 miles of United States coasts. The Coast Guard enforces fishing regulations and on occasion has seized foreign vessels in prohibited American waters.

As the agency responsible for enforcing United States laws at sea, the Coast Guard has been involved with problems of water pollution for many years. In 1971 it established an Office of Marine Environment and Systems at Coast Guard headquarters to administer all of its efforts in the field of environmental protection.

United States law prohibits the pollution of its waters and the Coast Guard works not only to apprehend those who break the law, but to prevent accidental spillage. When spillage does occur, the Coast Guard takes charge of clean-up activities. Coast Guard efforts to prevent water pollution begin with the enforcing of design and construction standards to reduce the accident potential of vessels carrying oil and other pollutants. Safety standards are also enforced in cargo handling on board ship and in port. The service encourages the development and use of equipment that will make navigation safer, such as the vessel bridge-to-bridge radio telephone communication system recently made mandatory for vessels navigating in United States waters. The Coast Guard's postaccident investigation indicated that the tanker collision in San Francisco Bay in January, 1971, which

A Coast Guard captain in dress blue uniform. The wings above the ribbons indicate that he is an aviator.

In 1972, for the first time in 25 years, the Coast Guard opened its basic training program to women reserves. Some of the new SPARs are shown here.

After two weeks of basic training at the Coast Guard Reserve Training Center at Yorktown, Virginia, SPARs line up for graduation ceremonies in August, 1972. Some of the sixty reservists who completed the training requested and received active duty assignments.

ENFORCING THE LAW IS THE COAST GUARD'S OLDEST MISSION

Pictured off Ketchikan, Alaska, are two of the Coast Guard's 40-foot steel utility boats. They were designed primarily for law enforcement work and for search and rescue efforts in moderate seas. The vessels carry the orange identification stripe that the Coast Guard adopted in 1967.

resulted in the spill of 840,000 gallons of oil, might have been avoided if there had been communication between the two tankers.

Coast Guard patrols watch for indications of debris, oil, and other polluting substances. In addition, the service's buoys and platforms are being equipped with special devices to determine the level of pollutants and to monitor changes in the environment.

Once a spill has occurred, the Coast Guard tries to control any pollution that results. To combat oil spills in open water where wind and sea action make control difficult, the Coast Guard has developed an air-droppable transfer system called ADAPTS to rapidly off-load a tanker that has grounded or ruptured into huge rubber bladders that can be towed away. a boom system to contain some open-sea oil spills has also been developed.

Because pollution problems are worldwide, the Coast Guard works with representatives of other maritime nations to curtail such practices as the discharge of oily wastes at sea.

Like law enforcement, search and rescue activities remain an important Coast Guard function. Modern cutters, patrol boats, aircraft, and communications have improved the service's capability in that field, which includes flood relief work as well as assistance to vessels and aircraft in distress at sea. The old lifeboat stations have evolved into rescue stations manned by crews of from twelve to twenty-five men. The stations maintain a constant readiness for rescue work in their assigned areas. If more help is needed, the coordination center of the Coast Guard district dispatches additional vessels and aircraft. When large amounts of equipment are required or extensive areas must be searched, the facilities of more than one district can be dispatched by the Coast Guard's two area commanders.

In 1970 the Coast Guard responded to more than 50,000 calls for help. Coast Guardsmen assisted 125,000 persons and saved 3,764 lives. The value of aircraft and vessels (including cargo) assisted came to $2.1 billion. And in 1971 they conducted 44,370 search and research missions and saved approximately 4,000 lives.

The Coast Guard's aids to navigation now serve air commerce and the armed forces as well as mariners, and facilities extend from the United States to the Western Pacific, the Arctic, Europe, and the Middle East. Loran stations account for the wide dispersal; most of the other aids are located along the coasts of the United States and on its inland waterways. These include lighthouses, offshore light structures, lightships, buoys, day beacons, short-range radio beacons, and fog signals. In all, the Coast Guard maintains more than 46,000 navigational aids.

Many thousands of small-boat owners have participated in the Boating Safety Program which the Coast Guard organized to make the operation of small craft both enjoyable and safe. In conjunction with its Boating Safety Program the service has worked to establish uniform and effective safety standards for recreational boats, to inform boat owners of the standards, and to ensure compliance through education and inspection.

The educational aspects of the Boating Safety Program are handled largely by the Coast Guard Auxiliary, a voluntary, nonmilitary organization of citizens owning small boats, aircraft, or radio stations. After training, members of the Auxiliary educate the boating public in safe practices and inspect small boats for proper safety equipment. They also volunteer their assistance to disabled boats, perform search and rescue missions, and patrol boat races and other marine events.

Members of the Coast Guard Auxiliary are United States citizens over seventeen years of age. They must own at least 25 percent of a motorboat, aircraft, or radio station, or qualify for membership because of special training or experience. They wear a distinctive uniform and, after passing an inspection, may fly the blue Auxiliary ensign from their boats. The ensign indicates that the boatman is competent and his vessel seaworthy and properly equipped.

Under the supervision of the Coast Guard, the Auxiliary is administered by elected and appointed officers. The basic Auxiliary unit is the flotilla, consisting of at least ten boats. Five or more flotillas are grouped together into divisions which, in turn, are grouped into districts corresponding to the Coast Guard districts.

Inaugurated in 1940 as a weather patrol to obtain information supplied in peacetime by merchant ships crossing the Atlantic, the Coast Guard's ocean station program now involves approximately thirty cutters and five Atlantic and one Pacific ocean stations. While on ocean station, usually for a three-week period, the cutters patrol a 44,000-square-mile area gathering meteorological information for the weather service and ships and aircraft en route. They also furnish other navigation aids to air and marine traffic. Ocean station cutters are equipped to collect oceanographic data as are Coast Guard icebreakers and the cutter assigned to the International Ice Patrol.

Cutters on ocean station are prepared to aid vessels and planes in distress and they have done so on

Winter patrol in the harbor area of Portland, Maine, has left ice on the harbor tug SHACKLE. In addition to towing, tugs similar to the SHACKLE are used by law enforcement boarding parties and for firefighting and icebreaking.

Operating out of Nantucket, Massachusetts, the patrol craft POINT BONITA is one of the "C" class of 82-footers designed for Coast Guard law enforcement and search and rescue work.

The Coast Guard's RED BIRCH, a 157-foot coastal tender, services aids to navigation along the California coast. Her other duties include law enforcement and search and rescue missions.

This 31-foot fiber glass boat was designed for Coast Guard port security duties. Boats of this type are assigned to Organized Reserve Port Security units for training purposes.

many occasions. Two notable instances were the rescue by the cutter *Bibb* of sixty-nine passengers from a flying boat forced down in the North Atlantic in 1947 and the cutter *Pontchartrain*'s rescue of thirty-one persons from a plane down in the Pacific in 1956.

Seven polar icebreakers and two on the Great Lakes make up the Coast Guard icebreaking fleet. In the polar regions icebreakers support military operations and participate in scientific missions. On the Great Lakes, iron ore shippers depend on the Coast Guard's icebreakers to expedite the movement of ore carriers each spring by opening a path through the ice. Reinforced tenders and harbor tugs function as icebreakers on the nation's northern rivers and harbors.

Although it operates as part of the Department of Transportation rather than the Department of Defense, the Coast Guard is a branch of the Armed Forces of the United States. Along with their other missions, its 38,000 officers and men maintain a readiness to function as a specialized service in the Navy in time of war. The Coast Guard's rank structure resembles that of the Navy, and Navy materials and methods are used in many training programs.

At the Navy's request, the Coast Guard dispatched seventeen of its highly maneuverable 82-foot patrol craft to South Vietnam in 1965 to protect that country's irregular coastline from infiltrators. The boats, along with an additional nine, formed what

was called Squadron One.

Coast Guardsmen assigned to Squadron One boarded and searched suspicious-looking craft and assisted ground forces with mortar fire. Five of the Coast Guard's high-endurance cutters were also sent to Southeast Asia to form Squadron Three. Operating from the Philippines, the cutters patrolled off the Vietnamese coast. After a year they were replaced by five others.

In Vietnam Coast Guardsmen operated electronic navigational aids, supervised the handling of explosives and other dangerous cargo, and assisted the United States Embassy with merchant marine problems.

Beginning in 1969 the Coast Guard turned the patrol boats of Squadron One over to the Republic of Vietnam Navy with four of the high-endurance cutters. However, Coast Guardsmen continued to advise the Vietnamese on port and merchant marine safety and aids to navigation.

Since the cutter *Massachusetts* took to the sea in 1791, the men of the Coast Guard have been ready when their expertise was needed for limited actions, such as that in Vietnam, or for a full-scale national emergency. Most of the time, however, Coast Guardsmen have enforced United States laws on its territorial waters, given protection to life and property at sea, and worked to improve maritime safety, and in doing so they have served their country well.

The Coast Guard seal, established by an executive order signed by President Dwight Eisenhower in 1957.

The identification stripe used on Coast Guard vessels, aircraft, signs, etc.

The Coast Guard emblem, as revised in 1967.

Under the watchful eye of a Coast Guard chief warrant officer, two crewmen repair the engine of a harbor patrol boat assigned to the Captain-of-the-Port Office, Baltimore, Maryland.

On patrol in New York Harbor, an amphibious helicopter flies above one of the Coast Guard's utility boats.

Representing the Coast Guard Captain-of-the-Port, a crew member inspects a dock warehouse in Baltimore, Maryland.

Marine safety begins with the plans for a new vessel. Here, two of the Coast Guard's marine inspectors check the architectural plans and a model for a merchant vessel to make sure it meets safety requirements. Plans must be approved by the Coast Guard before a merchant vessel can be built, altered, or repaired. During 1971 the Coast Guard reviewed over 30,000 such plans.

Engine equipment and machinery are among the items checked during the Coast Guard's periodic inspection of United States vessels and foreign vessels carrying passengers from United States ports. The Coast Guard inspector (right) is examining the seals on a boiler safety valve. During 1971, over 5,000 United States vessels were inspected for certification.

Boats, rafts, and other lifesaving equipment are thoroughly checked during a Coast Guard safety inspection. Here, a boat drill tests the competence of a passenger ship's crew.

Members of a Coast Guard boating safety detachment talk with the occupants of a pleasure craft. Coast Guardsmen on boating safety duty watch for violations of federal safety requirements.

The Coast Guard cutter STORIS has seized the Soviet factory fishing ship LAMUT off St. Matthew Island, Alaska, for violating the United States 12-mile-limit fishing agreement. The second of three Soviet vessels involved in the illegal fishing is at upper left. The three skippers were fined a total of $250,000, the largest fine ever levied by the United States, and released. The Soviet vessels were apprehended in January, 1972.

Whenever they discover floating debris, Coast Guardsmen destroy it or tow it from the path of other vessels. Here, they prepare to blow up a partially submerged vessel.

Under tow after running aground near San Juan, Puerto Rico, the broken tanker OCEAN EAGLE is spilling oil into the harbor. The Coast Guard seeks to prevent accidents like that of the OCEAN EAGLE which produced a spill of more than two million gallons of oil.

Among the victims of the wreck of the OCEAN EAGLE was this pelican being fed by Coast Guardsmen who cared for many oil-soaked birds at the San Juan Coast Guard base.

A closeup view of the barrier.

Using nontoxic and biodegradable soybean oil, the Coast Guard is testing its new containment barrier designed to protect coastal areas from offshore oil spills. The barrier can be deployed within four hours after oil is sighted.

Shown here in the form of a drawing is the Coast Guard's airborne pollution control system. A Coast Guard plane has just dropped two rubber tanks; three others are already taking on oil from the disabled tanker. The cutter in the foreground will tow the filled tanks to shore.

AN EXPANDING SEARCH AND RESCUE MISSION

A buoyant litter intended for high-line transfers or hoist pickups undergoes a Coast Guard test to determine if it will be a useful piece of rescue equipment.

Coast Guardsmen are testing a vinyl sponge buoyant mat for use as a rescue platform, one of the service's continuing tests of new types of search and rescue gear. The mat needs no inflation, can be rolled for storage and requires no maintenance.

Answering a request for assistance, the crew of a Coast Guard rescue craft passes a towline to a disabled cabin cruiser. The Coast Guard responded to over 40,000 calls for assistance during 1971.

Here, a Coast Guardsman plays the part of an unconscious man being raised in a rescue basket from a buoyant mat in a test of rescue gear.

This is one of the Coast Guard's older rescue stations, located at East Moriches, Long Island, New York.

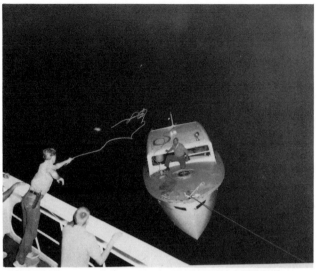

This photograph was taken in 1965 when numerous small boats were carrying Cuban refugees to the United States. The Coast Guard cutter (lower left) towed the stranded Cuban vessel to Key West, Florida.

The Cleveland Rescue Station on Lake Erie at the mouth of the Cuyahoga River was completed in 1940. It replaced an older station at Cleveland.

In 1966 one of the Coast Guard's amphibious helicopters landed in the Straits of Florida to rescue thirteen Cuban refugees who were attempting to reach the United States in a rowboat and a raft.

The Coast Guard's HH-52A amphibious helicopter was the first rotor-wing craft designed with a boat hull for water landings. It went into service in 1963. The HH-52A is powered by a gas turbine engine and equipped with a rescue platform that can be lowered from the cabin door for quick pickups.

One of the Coast Guard's pilots poses with the HH-3F helicopter.

The newer HH-3F twin-turbine amphibious helicopter, shown here demonstrating a basket rescue, is also used for border patrol, law enforcement, and research projects.

While on ocean station in the Atlantic in 1947, the cutter BIBB (shown here as she looked during World War II) rescued sixty-two passengers and a crew of seven from the flying boat BERMUDA SKY QUEEN. The BIBB's crew used small boats and rafts to bring all those aboard the plane through towering waves to the safety of the cutter.

When a Japan Air Lines jet crashed into the bay off San Francisco International Airport in 1968, Coast Guard boats and life rafts rescued 108 persons.

Coast Guardsmen in a rubber raft (right) completed the rescue of eight men from a crippled fishing vessel off Newfoundland moments before the vessel sank. The Coast Guardsmen were from the cutter CASTLE ROCK which answered a call for help while en route to her ocean station in February, 1967.

One of the Coast Guard's amphibious helicopters is lifting three crewmen to safety as their fishing trawler ORIENTAL sinks off Nags Head, North Carolina, during a winter storm in 1969.

Crewmen in the cutter YAKUTAT rescued four of nine men stranded on the bow section of the tanker FORT MERCER which broke up in a severe Atlantic storm in February, 1952. The Coast Guardsmen are shown here working with the rubber rafts used in the rescue effort.

When this photograph was taken, the bow section of the FORT MERCER was sinking into the sea. The cutters ACUSHNET and EASTWIND rescued twenty-one men from the stern section of the FORT MERCER; thirteen others remained with the stern while it was towed to shore.

One of the Coast Guard's early amphibians landed to rescue the crew of a boat that caught fire off Cape May, New Jersey, in 1935. Amphibians continue to play an important role in Coast Guard rescues.

While the FORT MERCER rescue was under way, Coast Guardsmen from Chatham Lifeboat Station on the Massachusetts coast were removing thirty-two survivors from the stern section of the tanker PENDLETON which broke up in the same storm. This is the bow section of the PENDLETON which contained no survivors.

The HU-16E Albatross has seen many years of service as a Coast Guard primary search and rescue aircraft. The twin-engine, all-weather plane can operate from land or water bases.

Its long range and large cargo compartment make the HC-130 Hercules a useful Coast Guard search and rescue plane. It can also be used as a communications center to coordinate rescue operations involving several aircraft and surface vessels.

After maneuvering the cutter COOS BAY (lower left) into position, Coast Guardsmen have successfully thrown a line to the British ship AMBASSADOR, sinking in an Atlantic storm with twelve crewmen still on board. The COOS BAY was returning to Portland, Maine, from ocean station duty when she answered the AMBASSADOR's call for help.

High seas have increased the distance between the two vessels, but rescue operations continue in this photograph of the AMBASSADOR and the COOS BAY. The COOS BAY rescued eleven of the twelve survivors on the AMBAS-SADOR. The twelfth man drowned while being pulled through the waves to the cutter.

Although her primary duty was servicing aids to navigation, the Coast Guard buoy tender SHRUB was ready to help a ship grounded during a storm off the Massachusetts coast. The SHRUB pulled the ship clear at high tide.

Some of the Coast Guard's vessels are equipped for fire fighting and offer valuable assistance when fires break out at waterfront facilities. Here, Coast Guardsmen battle a fire that burned a pier at the Norfolk Navy Yard Annex in 1945.

When the British tanker ALVA CAPE collided with the American tanker TEXACO MASSACHUSETTS off Staten Island, New York, in 1966, Coast Guard amphibious helicopters helped pick up survivors. The Coast Guard also dispatched tugs and utility boats to the collision scene.

The 210-foot cutter DEPENDABLE, with a helicopter on her flight deck, stands by at the scene of an oil platform fire off the Louisiana coast. The cutter was dispatched from Panama City, Florida, her home port, to monitor the fire and to provide rescue services if they were needed.

Coast Guard rescue craft go out in the roughest weather. This 52-foot motor lifeboat was photographed off the Oregon coast where dangerous surf conditions are frequent.

It was photographed here in San Francisco Bay on a calm day, but the Coast Guard's 44-foot steel motor lifeboat has rolled over in high waves, righted itself and continued with engines running. The craft was especially designed for rescue work in rough water.

A crewman on the cutter DALLAS throws a grappling hook over the side. The 378-foot DALLAS, a sister ship of the SHERMAN, was named for Alexander Dallas, Secretary of the Treasury in President James Madison's Cabinet.

Long-range search and rescue missions are handled by the Coast Guard's new 378-foot cutters which also perform ocean station patrol, oceanographic research, and meteorology duties. The SHERMAN (above) named for John Sherman, Secretary of the Treasury from 1877 until 1881, was commissioned in 1968. She carries the latest rescue equipment, which may include a helicopter on her flight deck.

Flood relief work is part of the Coast Guard's search and rescue mission. These Coast Guardsmen were called in after a serious flood in Missouri in 1950.

When hurricane Betsy devastated the Louisiana coast in 1965, eleven Coast Guard helicopters flew 140 sorties during which they rescued 1,144 persons and transported twenty-two medics. Here, a helicopter scoops up a man stranded on a rooftop.

In the aftermath of tropical storm Agnes which brought torrential rains to the eastern part of the United States in June, 1972, 150 Coast Guardsmen, with boats and helicopters, were rushed to Pennsylvania where the Susquehanna River had flooded large areas. This picture was taken near Wilkes-Barre.

From the door of a helicopter flying along the Mississippi coast, a crewman surveys the damage done by hurricane Camille in August, 1969. Coast Guard helicopters evacuated sick and injured persons and brought in medical supplies.

Coast Guardsmen from a Third U.S. Coast Guard District boating safety detachment evacuate Pennsylvania flood victims.

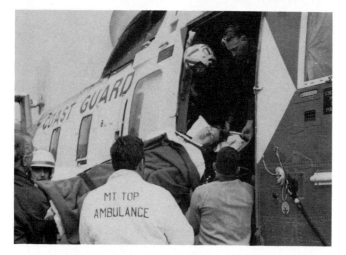

Coast Guard aircraft flew a total of 85 hours in the Pennsylvania flood area. Here, a heart attack victim is moved from a helicopter to an ambulance. Coast Guard helicopters also transported medical teams.

In addition to taking care of buoys, the Coast Guard's buoy tenders deliver supplies to remote light stations and lightships and service unattended lights. They also do patrol and rescue work. This is the 132-foot tender WHITE SAGE.

This loran transmitting station on Yap in the Caroline Islands is one of several stations operated by the Coast Guard in the Pacific.

The Coast Guard uses its C-123s to carry supplies to its far-flung loran stations. The C-123 has a large cargo compartment and it can land and take off from improvised fields.

At Port Clarence, Alaska, the top of the loran antenna tower is 1,300 feet above the ground. It is one of the tallest of the Coast Guard's loran towers.

**THE COAST GUARD'S OCEAN STATION VESSELS
PROVIDE VALUABLE SERVICES**

After World War II the cutter CAMPBELL, pictured here in the harbor at Argentia, Newfoundland, was assigned to the one Atlantic ocean station then in operation. There are now five ocean stations along Atlantic air and shipping routes.

No matter how bad the weather, a cutter remains on ocean station until relieved by another cutter or called away by an emergency. This is the ESCANABA patrolling ocean station Delta, some 650 miles southeast of Newfoundland.

Since they began to enter service in the late 1960s, the Coast Guard's 378-foot high endurance cutters have taken their turn at ocean station duty. This is the BOUTWELL, the fifth of fifteen cutters in the new class that will be named for Secretaries of the Treasury and Coast Guard heroes. The vessels are equipped with the latest electronic, meteorological, and oceanographic gear.

For Coast Guardsmen, ocean station duty can mean many days of high seas and cold winds. Here, the cutter PONT-CHARTRAIN wallows in the trough of a following sea on ocean station Bravo.

After a winter storm, a cutter on ocean station can be completely covered with ice.

Collecting weather data is an important part of ocean station duty. Here, Coast Guardsmen launch a weather-balloon-borne radiosonde transmitter that will relay information on upper atmospheric pressures, humidities, temperatures, and wind velocities.

Because ice endangers the crew and affects the performance of the cutter, it must be removed, a tedious job that requires the use of pick and shovel.

A Coast Guardsman prepares to lower a Nansen bottle into the sea to collect a water sample. Cutters assigned to the Ocean Station Project are equipped with laboratories and the gear needed to conduct scientific studies involving water samples and marine life.

BREAKING ICE FOR THE FEDERAL GOVERNMENT

With her diesel-electric engines going full blast, the Coast Guard icebreaker NORTHWIND charges into the Antarctic ice during the 1946–47 Operation High Jump. The NORTH-WIND, commissioned in 1945, was on loan to Navy Task Force 68 for the Antarctic expedition. The powerful ice-breaker was designed with large tanks on her port and starboard sides. Pumping water back and forth produced a rocking effect that helped the vessel move through the ice. The NORTHWIND carried 1⅝ inches of extra hull plating.

The NORTHWIND's pontoon-equipped helicopter was photographed as it left the icebreaker's deck to scout for leads in the ice pack. In the background are the Operation High Jump vessels MERRICK, YANCY, and MT. OLYMPUS, thin-hulled ships that depended on the NORTH-WIND to open a passage through the ice.

Caught in a field of dangerous floating ice, the YANCY had to be towed to safety by the NORTHWIND (foreground).

From the NORTHWIND's deck, a member of the expedition recovers a bathythermograph that was used to record water temperatures.

In addition to icebreaking, the NORTHWIND participated in Operation High Jump's scientific studies. Here, a coring tube is lowered over the side for a bottom sample. The NORTHWIND carried over four miles of cable on her tube-cable spool (lower left).

The NORTHWIND's J2F amphibian has landed after a reconnaissance flight. It will be towed to the icebreaker and raised to her deck.

A cargo net loaded with mail and supplies for Operation High Jump moves from the Navy's PHILIPPINE SEA to the NORTHWIND (on left).

Destined for the National Zoological Park in Washington, D.C., a 65-pound penguin had to be moved to safety when a storm threatened the NORTHWIND on her return journey from the Antarctic.

Crewmen on the NORTHWIND are splicing a towing cable which broke while the Coast Guard icebreaker was towing the MERRICK after that vessel was disabled by a broken rudder post. The NORTHWIND towed the MERRICK 1,400 miles to New Zealand.

During the Joint United States–Canadian Beaufort Sea Expedition in the summer of 1954, the NORTHWIND (in background) made the first west to east passage through the previously impenetrable McClure Strait. Here, expedition members erect a mast for a micrometeorology study.

In this 1952 photo Baffin Island Eskimos are examining a helicopter from the EASTWIND, another of the Coast Guard's Wind-class icebreakers. When the EASTWIND was stopped by solid ice, her commanding officer flew to Baffin Island to arrange for sledges and dogs to transport a scientific team and its equipment to test sites along the coast.

The SOUTHWIND, a sister ship of the NORTHWIND, was commissioned during World War II and turned over to the Navy.

The EASTWIND's mascot, a 4-foot emperor penguin, posed for his picture at McMurdo Sound.

During Operation Deep Freeze I (1955–56) the EASTWIND traveled to the Antarctic. Here, the icebreaker is cutting a channel in McMurdo Sound.

After more than two months in the Antarctic during the 1960 Operation Deep Freeze, the EASTWIND is unloading supplies for wintering-over personnel before departing for Boston, her home port. At lower left is a helicopter damaged during unloading operations. It was returned to the United States aboard the EASTWIND.

Coast Guardsmen can expect boat drill no matter where they are. This boat was launched from the EASTWIND during one of the icebreaker's trips to the Antarctic.

The EASTWIND leads the way through the Antarctic ice to McMurdo Base during Operation Deep Freeze in 1963. The black spots on the ice are seals.

On a mission to save a starving Eskimo village, the Coast Guard icebreaker WESTWIND cuts a path through Greenland's Melville Bay for a Danish supply ship. For their part in the successful delivery of food and fuel in the fall of 1964, the crew of the WESTWIND received the Coast Guard Unit Commendation Award.

Photographed from the deck of the buoy tender SPAR, the cutters STORIS (on right) and BRAMBLE make their way through the ice of Simpson Strait en route to Bellot Strait in August, 1957. Bellot Strait proved to be a practical deepwater route for the long-sought Northwest Passage across northern North America. The three Coast Guard vessels were the first to make the transit.

The 180-foot buoy tender SPAR was named for the Coast Guard's Women Reserves. Her hull is reinforced for ice-breaking.

Assigned to the 1968 Operation Deep Freeze, the ice-breaker BURTON ISLAND works to keep a channel open through McMurdo Sound to the Deep Freeze base at Hut Point. The picture was taken from another icebreaker, the GLACIER. Both vessels were transferred from the Navy to the Coast Guard when the latter organization was made the chief icebreaking agency for the federal government.

While the 310-foot GLACIER waits in the Weddell Sea, scientists and crewmen from the icebreaker are collecting water samples and specimens of the organic life beneath the Antarctic ice. A shelter tent can be seen at left.

The device being lowered over the GLACIER's side is a Van Ween Grab. It was used to collect sediment samples from the bottom of the Weddell Sea.

A crewman from the GLACIER hands a Van Dorn bottle to a diver who will use it to collect water samples at various levels of light penetration beneath the Weddell Sea ice.

In another of the oceanographic surveys conducted by the GLACIER, a current-meter buoy was left adrift to measure the direction and speed of water in the Ross Sea. Here, a crewman retrieves the buoy.

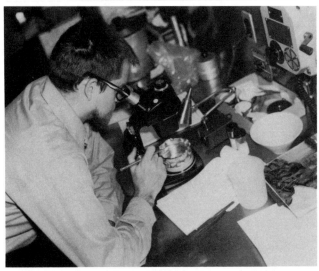

In the GLACIER's well-equipped laboratory, a scientist studies a specimen taken from the bottom of the Weddell Sea.

Two of the Coast Guard's icebreakers, the GLACIER (leading) and the EASTWIND (on right) were escorting a Navy fuel tanker in ice-covered McMurdo Sound when this photo was taken. In the right foreground is a cross erected to one of the members of Robert Scott's first Antarctic expedition.

When the tanker-icebreaker MANHATTAN made her historic voyage to Prudhoe Bay near the newly discovered oilfields on Alaska's northern slope in 1969, one of her escorts was the venerable Coast Guard icebreaker NORTH-WIND. Here, the NORTHWIND's helicopter returns after searching for a passage through the ice.

In 1943, after an exceptionally cold winter and spring, several vessels became locked in the Lake Erie ice near Buffalo. The small vessel on the right is the Coast Guard icebreaker CITRUS coming to the aid of the B. LYMAN SMITH.

On the MANHATTAN's (in background) return trip from Prudhoe Bay, the Coast Guard icebreaker STATEN ISLAND (foreground) helped her through the frozen Arctic waterways.

The Coast Guard's 290-foot Great Lakes icebreaker MACK-INAW leads four freighters through the frozen St. Mary's River. The vessels are en route from Duluth to Chicago. Each year the icebreaking services of the MACKINAW are used to extend the Great Lakes shipping season. The MACKINAW was commissioned in 1945.

COAST GUARDSMEN IN VIETNAM

Five of the 82-foot patrol craft assigned to Coast Guard Squadron One arrive in Vietnam in 1965 for duty with the U.S. Navy's Coastal Surveillance Force. The 82-footers were shipped to the Philippines on transports and traveled from there to Vietnam under their own power. Each craft was manned by two officers and eight men.

Two loaders and a telephone talker man an 81 mm. mortar on the 82-foot cutter POINT COMFORT off the coast of South Vietnam.

On patrol off the South Vietnamese coast, the crew of the
POINT COMFORT has stopped a junk to make sure it
carries no supplies intended for the Viet Cong.

Aboard one of the 82-foot patrol craft on duty in South
Vietnam, a Coast Guardsman loads an 81 mm. mortar.

The 82-footer POINT LEAGUE (foreground) has forced
an enemy trawler into shallow water. The trawler is burning following an explosion. Coast Guardsmen removed
arms and supplies from the trawler.

The 311-foot BERING STRAIT sports a new coat of gray paint, the first step in her Vietnamization. She was one of four cutters turned over to the Republic of Vietnam Navy in 1971.

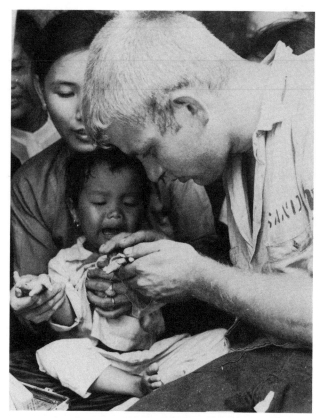

Between patrols many Coast Guardsmen carried out goodwill missions. Here, a crewman from the POINT GLOVER treats the injured hand of a Vietnamese child.

Pictured here still flying the American flag and painted the traditional Coast Guard white, the cutter CASTLE ROCK was transferred to the Republic of Vietnam Navy in December, 1971. Both the BERING STRAIT and the CASTLE ROCK were commissioned in 1944 and served as Navy seaplane tenders before becoming Coast Guard vessels.

The U.S. Coast Guard Academy

Because the Coast Guard is a small organization with only 38,000 officers and men, the smallest of the armed forces, it places a premium upon leadership. Relatively early in their careers Coast Guard officers are called upon to assume command responsibility in one of the many units into which the service is divided. Preparing them for this responsibility, and for added responsibilities in later years, is the function of the Coast Guard Academy.

Many of the Coast Guard's first officers learned their trade in the Continental Navy. When the Navy was disbanded after the Revolutionary War, they brought their ability to handle men and ships to Alexander Hamilton's cutter fleet, then known as the Revenue Marine. Other early Revenue Marine officers came from the merchant marine. Politics played a big part in appointment and advancement in those days. Once appointed, an officer retained his assignment and received promotions as long as he remained in favor with the local collector of customs, a situation that invited abuse.

Morale was low in the Revenue Marine when

Louis McLane became Secretary of the Treasury in 1831. After an investigation of the organization's personnel problems, he announced a new policy: "With a view to greater efficiency in the cutter service in future, vacancies will be filled by promotions from among the officers in that service, when that shall be found preferable to other appointments, having regards to fitness as well as seniority."

McLane's stand helped matters somewhat and reforms were continued by other secretaries of the Treasury, notably John C. Spencer, who, in 1843, set up the Revenue Marine Bureau in Washington to centralize control of the service. He also instituted a system of original appointments only in the grade of third lieutenant and promotion by examination before a board of officers. In 1845, Congress, in the act establishing an engineer corps for the Revenue Marine, included the provision that no one "be appointed to the office of Captain, first, second, and third lieutenant of any revenue cutter, who does not adduce competent proof of proficiency and skill in seamanship and navigation."

Carrying the flag of the United States, the Coast Guard colors and the Academy Corps of Cadets flag, a color guard parades on the Coast Guard Academy's New London campus.

The schooner JAMES C. DOBBIN, the first school ship of what was to become the Coast Guard Academy, is shown here as depicted in a watercolor by C. J. A. Wilson. Before becoming a school ship, the DOBBIN served for twenty-four years as a Revenue Service cutter on the Atlantic coast. She was sold at auction for $5,166.00 in 1881.

More than thirty years passed before Congress moved to establish a training program for young men who wished to become officers in the Revenue Cutter Service. In the meantime, the Revenue Marine Bureau had ceased to exist and politically inspired appointments and promotions again became the rule. The demands of the Civil War reversed this trend, however, and by 1865 a movement to reinstate centralized control of the Cutter Service was under way. Congress formally established a Revenue Marine Division in the Treasury Department in 1875.

Beginning in 1869 the Revenue Cutter Service took steps to remove undesirable officers from its rolls, many of them men acquired during the service's Civil War expansion. Seven of nineteen captains and thirty-three of 103 lieutenants were released. Those that remained were awarded a rank determined by their qualifications. Moreover, regulations were adopted to eliminate political influence in appointments, promotions, and assignments. Appointments could be made only in the grade of third lieutenant or second assistant engineer, and candidates were required to have a certain amount of practical experience and to pass physical and professional examinations.

The next step was a school in which the Revenue Cutter Service could train its own officer candidates. At the request of the Service, Congress authorized a two-year cadet training program in 1876.

In December of 1876, nineteen young men between the ages of eighteen and twenty-five appeared before an examining board to demonstrate their knowledge of arithmetic, geography, and English. In addition, the candidates were graded on their "general apititude." Nine failed the written examination and a tenth was failed in general aptitude. According to the examining board, he made an unfavorable impression "by his general deportment and by his manifest disposition to prevaricate."

Because experience aboard a sailing vessel was deemed the best way to prepare a young man for service at sea, the Revenue Cutter Service's first class of cadets reported to the schooner *Dobbin* in May, 1877. The *Dobbin* had been fitted out as a school ship under the command of Captain J. A. Henriques, one of the service's most able officers.

During each of their two years at the School of Instruction, cadets were to spend one term at sea and two terms ashore. While at sea they received practical training in seamanship, navigation, signals, and "exercises aloft." After the *Dobbin* tied up at New Bedford, Massachusetts, in October, the cadets began academic studies that included algebra, geometry,

Photographed under full sail is the SALMON P. CHASE, the School of Instruction's second school ship. Before she was remodeled to accommodate twenty-five cadets, the CHASE contained six staterooms, each equipped with two berths, a washstand, and clothing lockers.

trigonometry, philosophy, astronomy, history, French, English, customs law, navigation law, and international law. A drill loft and a rigging shed served as classrooms.

Before the class of 1879 graduated, the *Dobbin* was replaced by the *Salmon P. Chase,* a bark-rigged vessel that had been especially designed as a school ship. The *Chase* had accommodations for twelve cadets and, like the *Dobbin,* she tied up at New Bedford each winter while the cadets pursued their studies ashore.

Upon graduation cadets received commissions as third lieutenants in the Revenue Cutter Service. The School of Instruction provided most of the service's new third lieutenants until 1890 when it was forced to close because there were so few openings for beginning officers. The Revenue Cutter Service had no provisions for the retirement of its older officers, with the predictable result that few retired un-

less compelled to do so by serious illness, and promotions were held up all down the line. The few openings that occurred each year were filled by surplus Naval Academy graduates until 1894 when the expansion of the Navy absorbed all Academy graduates. In 1895 Congress passed legislation retiring some Revenue Service officers and the ensuing promotions left many openings in the grade of third lieutenant. To fill the vacancies, the School of Instruction resumed operations.

The School of Instruction continued to offer two years of training, but now only candidates who had completed their general scholastic work were admitted. As cadets they concentrated on technical and professional subjects. The *Chase,* lengthened forty feet to make room for a total of twenty-five cadets, returned to service as the school's training ship, moving with the cadets to various southern ports in the winter because the school's former winter quarters at

One of the Revenue Cutter Service's cadets posed for this photograph in 1885.

The School of Instruction Class of 1896 was photographed on board the CHASE with school officials (on right).

New Bedford were no longer available. In 1900, however, the School of Instruction for the Revenue Cutter Service opened winter quarters at Arundel Cove, Maryland.

To better prepare officers for duty in a Revenue Cutter Service whose missions were expanding and whose vessels were becoming more complex, Congress, in 1903, extended the training period at the School of Instruction from two to three years, allowing more time for the study of scientific subjects. In 1906 a six-months cadetship (later extended to a full year) was inaugurated for engineers who had previously been commissioned directly from civilian life. They took indoctrinational courses and studied advanced engineering. A new training ship, the *Itasca*, replaced the *Chase* in 1907. The *Itasca*, powered by steam with auxiliary sail, gave the engineering cadets

practical experience in ship operation.

Although the Revenue Cutter Service's cadet corps was not large, classes ranging in size from ten to twenty young men, the facilities at Arundel Cove proved inadequate and generally unsuitable for school purposes. Better quarters were located at Fort Trumbull at New London, Connecticut, and in 1910 the School of Instruction moved to its new home. In 1914, following improvements in the curriculum, the Revenue Cutter Service changed the name of its school to Revenue Cutter Academy. A year later it became the United States Coast Guard Academy.

During World War I, the Coast Guard Academy, like the other service academies, graduated its classes early, as it was to do again during World War II. The disruption during World War I was short, however, and the cadets soon resumed their three-year pro-

In 1906, twenty-six cadets (in white visor hats) sailed on an Atlantic cruise aboard the CHASE. The CHASE's officers are seated in the front row.

Pre-World War I cadets train for their future role as officers in the Revenue Cutter Service, then and now the nation's smallest military force.

gram of studies at New London and summer cruises aboard the Academy's training ship. The postwar training ship was the *Alexander Hamilton*, a steam-propelled auxiliary three-masted barkentine that had begun her career in 1898 as a Navy gunboat. She could accommodate up to a hundred cadets who slept in hammocks.

A training ship as large as the *Hamilton* had become necessary because the Academy was growing, so much so that Fort Trumbull was badly overcrowded. In 1929, after repeated requests from the Coast Guard, Congress appropriated $1,750,000 for "such buildings as [the Secretary of the Treasury] may deem necessary for the purposes of the United States Coast Guard Academy."

In 1932 cadets and instructors moved to a new location on the west bank of the Thames River in New London. Shortly before the move, the length of the Academy course was extended to four years. Line, or regular, and engineering cadets no longer pursued separate programs; all cadets studied both line and engineering subjects. The curriculum was revised to meet the standards set by the nation's civilian colleges, and in 1940 the Academy was accredited by the Association of American Universities and authorized to grant the degree of bachelor of science.

Today, approximately 1,100 cadets are enrolled in the Coast Guard Academy. They come from every state of the Union, with a few special cadets coming from the American republics and the Republic of the

These five young men made up the Coast Guard Academy Class of 1923. They are standing at the entrance to Fort Trumbull.

Philippines. Appointments to the Academy are made solely on the basis of an annual nationwide competition; there are no congressional appointments and no geographic quotas.

To qualify for an appointment to the Coast Guard Academy, a young man must be between seventeen and twenty-two years of age, a United States citizen, unmarried, of good character, and he must meet certain physical and scholastic requirements. If he is accepted as a cadet, he has his choice of thirteen academic options: general engineering, ocean engineering, electrical engineering, nuclear engineering, marine engineering, civil engineering, mathematics, computer science, chemistry, ocean science, economics/management, physics, and his-

tory/government. Athletics and military training are required of all cadets.

During their four years at the Academy, cadets take three cruises of about two weeks each on the training ship *Eagle*, a three-masted auxiliary bark, and two seven-week cruises on Coast Guart cutters. On the cutters the cadets study gunnery, antisubmarine warfare procedures, engineering, and cutter operation.

While he is at the Academy a cadet receives one half the base pay of an ensign with less than two years' service. This is used to pay for uniforms, textbooks, and other training expenses.

When he graduates, a cadet is awarded a bachelor of science degree and a commission as ensign in

It was graduation day at the Coast Guard Academy when this photograph of the cadet company was taken in 1924.

The Coast Guard Academy at Fort Trumbull, New London, Connecticut, as photographed from the air in 1927.

the United States Coast Guard. He is obligated to serve for five years as a commissioned officer in an organization that is like no other in the range of its functions, combining as it does such varied activities as saving lives, protecting property, enforcing the law, scientific investigation, and preserving national security. The Coast Guard Academy has prepared him to take his place as a leader in this unique organization.

The formal statement of the Academy's mission was drafted in 1929 by Superintendent Harry C. Hamlet. It remains in effect today.

"To graduate young men with sound bodies, stout hearts, and alert minds, with a liking for the sea and its lore, and with that high sense of honor, loyalty, and obedience which goes with trained initiative and leadership; well grounded in seamanship, the sciences, and the amenities and strong in the resolve to be worthy of the traditions of commissioned officers in the United States Coast Guard in the service of their country and humanity."

An aerial view of the Coast Guard Academy which now occupies a 100-acre site on the
Thames River in New London. The large building at the left is Chase Hall, the cadets'
quarters. The training ship EAGLE is tied up at a dock in the background.

In 1960 an extension was added to Chase Hall to house additional cadets' quarters, a store, barbershop, kitchen, dining room, and other facilities.

The cadet dining room in the Chase Hall extension.

Satterlee Hall houses classrooms and laboratories.

This photograph of cadets marching in review at the Coast Guard Academy was taken in 1948.

Douglas A. Munro Hall, named for the Coast Guard's World War II Medal of Honor winner,
serves as a barracks for enlisted men stationed at the Academy.

Stately Hamilton Hall is the Coast Guard Academy's administration building.

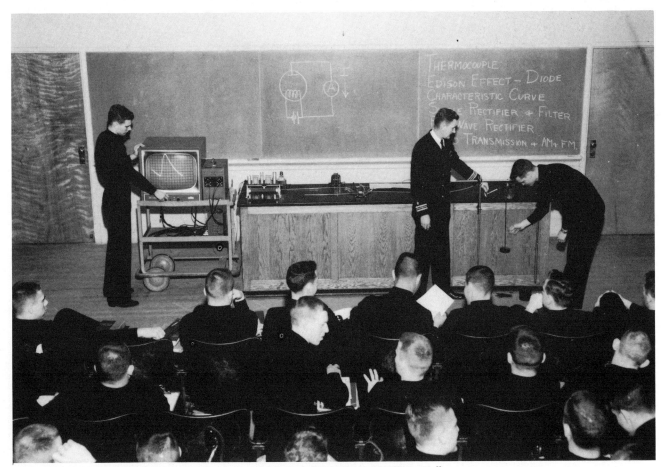

Thermodynamics is the subject these cadets are studying in a classroom in McAllister Hall, the Coast Guard Academy's applied science and engineering building.

McAllister Hall houses a subcritical nuclear reactor. Here, cadets conduct an experiment using the reactor.

The Coast Guard Academy has its own observatory.

Billard Hall, with its well-equipped gymnasium, is the center of the Academy's athletic program.

A cadet and his instructor are working out an engineering problem relating to naval architecture. All cadets at the Coast Guard Academy study naval architecture.

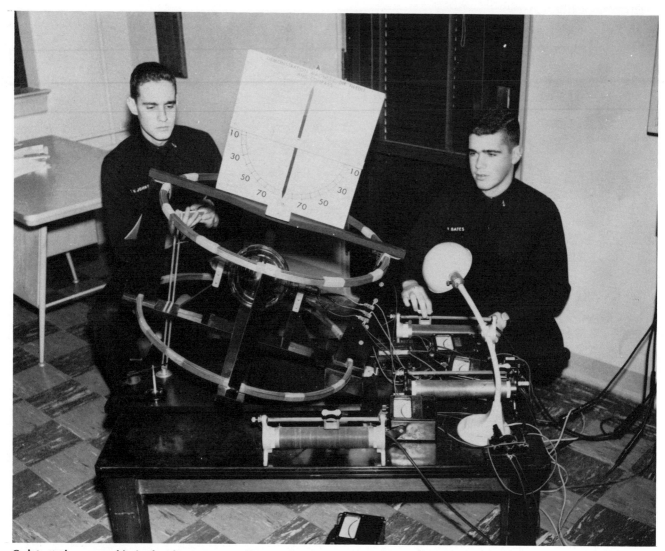

Cadets study seamanship in the classroom as well as on training ships. These fourth-year men are working with a demonstration dip needle and compass.

Memorial chapel at the Coast Guard Academy.

A chapel window depicts freedom of speech.

In this winter photograph of the Coast Guard Academy campus, the parade ground is at the left. The building in the background is Hamilton Hall.

MASTERING THE ART OF SEAMANSHIP ON THE EAGLE

Acquired from Germany as part of war reparations, the 295-foot EAGLE has been the Coast Guard Academy's training ship since 1946. The vessel is equipped with a 700 h.p. auxiliary diesel engine, but operates under sail 80 percent of the time. During cruises on the EAGLE and on the Coast Guard's modern cutters cadets learn basic seamanship.

Learning to handle the wheel. In the background cadets stand ready for man-overboard drill.

Shooting the sun, an important lesson in navigation.

Plotting the course of a plane flying over the EAGLE.

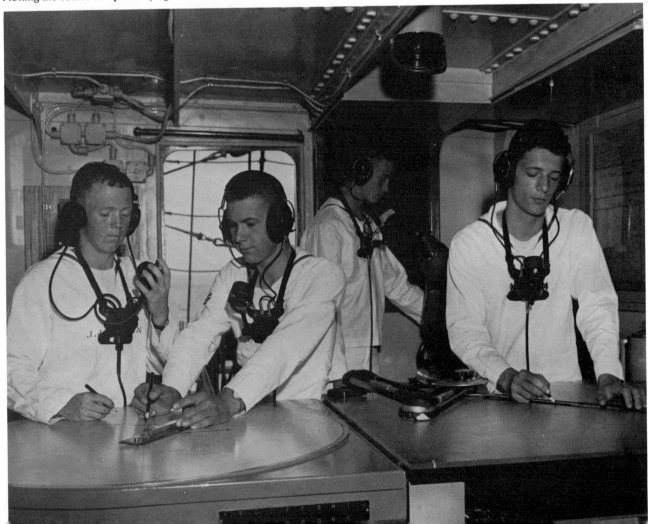

Climbing the ratlines to unfurl the EAGLE's sails.

Sure footwork on the yardarms.

Moving out on the EAGLE's bowsprit to secure the lines of the headsails.

Newly commissioned ensigns in the U.S. Coast Guard happily pick up hats and shoulder boards on graduation day.

In 1964 President Lyndon Johnson presented the Coast Guard Academy's top honor graduate with his commission scroll and a mounted set of ensign's boards.

Semper Paratus

Official U.S. Coast Guard Marching Song

Words and music by CAPTAIN FRANCIS SALTUS VAN BOSKERCK, USCG

Verse

From Aztec shore to Arctic Zone,
To Europe and Far East,
The Flag is carried by our ships
In times of war and peace;
And never have we struck it yet
In spite of foemen's might,
Who cheered our crews and cheered again
For showing how to fight.

CHORUS

So here's the Coast Guard marching song,
We sing on land or sea.
Through surf and storm and howling gale,
High shall our purpose be.
"Semper Paratus" is our guide,
Our fame, our glory, too,
To fight to save or fight and die!
Aye! Coast Guard, we are for you.

2nd Verse

SURVEYOR and NARCISSUS,
The EAGLE and DISPATCH,
The HUDSON and the TAMPA,
The names are hard to match;
From Barrow's shores to Paraguay,
Great Lakes or ocean's wave,
The Coast Guard fought through storms and winds
To punish or to save.

3rd Verse

Aye, we've been "Always Ready"
To do, to fight, or die,
Write glory to the shield we wear
In letters to the sky.
To sink the foe or save the maimed
Our mission and our pride,
We'll carry on 'til Kingdom Come
Ideals for which we've died.

INSIGNIA OF THE UNITED STATES COAST GUARD

COMMISSIONED

O-10	O-9	O-8	O-7	O-6	O-5	O-4	O-3	O-2	O-1
ADMIRAL	VICE ADMIRAL	REAR ADMIRAL (UPPER HALF)	REAR ADMIRAL (LOWER HALF)	CAPTAIN	COMMANDER	LIEUTENANT COMMANDER	LIEUTENANT	LIEUTENANT JUNIOR GRADE	ENSIGN

CAP DEVICES

OFFICER AND CHIEF WARRANT

CHIEF PETTY OFFICER

WARRANT

WARRANT

CHIEF WARRANT OFFICER W-4	CHIEF WARRANT OFFICER W-3	CHIEF WARRANT OFFICER W-2	WARRANT OFFICER W-1

UNITED STATES COAST GUARD
SLEEVE INSIGNIA DESIGN

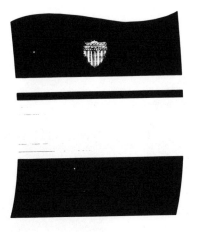

Rear Admiral

Commander

Chief Warrant, W-4

Warrant, W-1

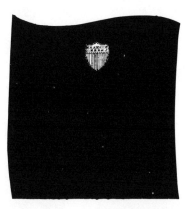

Chief Petty Officers
and Enlisted Women
Right Coat Sleeve

Enlisted Men Below CPO
Right Sleeve

Cadet
First Class

Cadet
Second Class

Cadet
Third Class

Cadet
Fourth Class

235

UNITED STATES COAST GUARD
SHOULDER MARK DESIGN

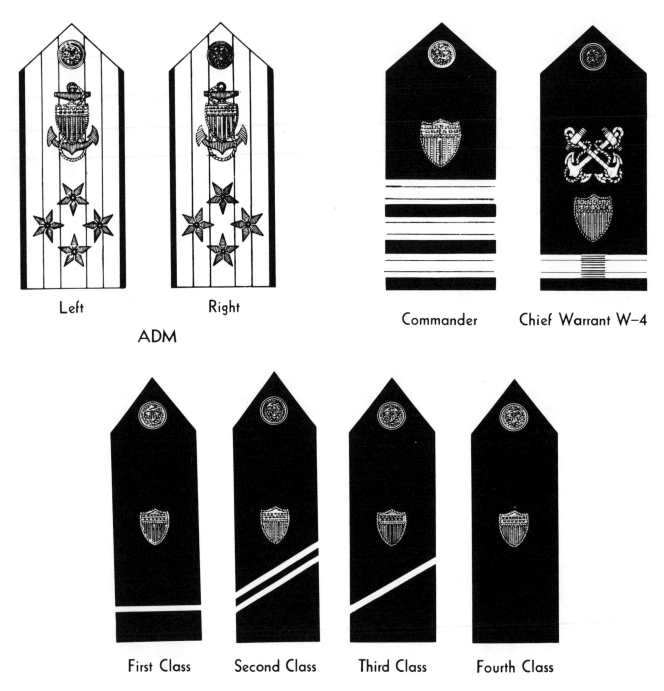

Left   Right

ADM

Commander   Chief Warrant W–4

First Class   Second Class   Third Class   Fourth Class

Coast Guard Academy Cadets

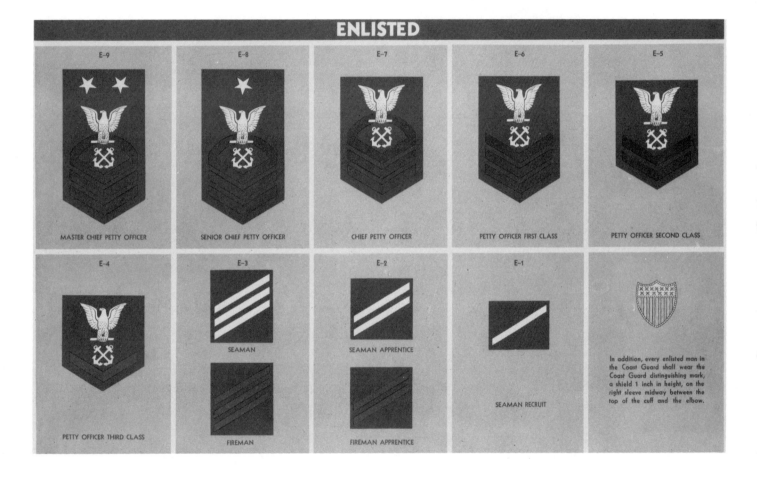

ENLISTED

E-9	E-8	E-7	E-6	E-5
MASTER CHIEF PETTY OFFICER	SENIOR CHIEF PETTY OFFICER	CHIEF PETTY OFFICER	PETTY OFFICER FIRST CLASS	PETTY OFFICER SECOND CLASS

E-4	E-3	E-2	E-1	
PETTY OFFICER THIRD CLASS	SEAMAN / FIREMAN	SEAMAN APPRENTICE / FIREMAN APPRENTICE	SEAMAN RECRUIT	

In addition, every enlisted man in the Coast Guard shall wear the Coast Guard distinguishing mark, a shield 1 inch in height, on the right sleeve midway between the top of the cuff and the elbow.

UNITED STATES COAST GUARD
CAP DEVICES

Commissioned Officers
and
Commissioned Warrant Officers

Warrant Officer
W–1

Cadet

Chief Petty
Officer

Enlisted
Women

CHIEF PETTY OFFICER COLLAR INSIGNIA

Chief Petty
Officer

Senior Chief
Petty Officer

Master Chief
Petty Officer

238

UNITED STATES COAST GUARD

FULL DRESS BAND UNIFORM INSIGNIA

Cap Device

Sleeve Loops

Sleeve Insignia

Chin Strap

DISTINCTIVE MARKINGS

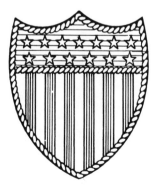

Shield
(Metallic)

Button
(Metallic)

Shield
(Embroidered)

U.S. COAST GUARD COMMANDANTS SINCE 1790

1790 to 1843	Cutters were administered by Treasury through local Collectors of Customs.
1843 to 1848	Captain Alexander V. Frazer, Chief, Revenue Marine Bureau of Treasury Dept.
1848 to 1849	Captain Richard Evans, Chief, Revenue Marine Bureau.
1849 to 1871	Cutters again administered by Treasury through local Collectors of Customs.
Feb. 1, 1871, to c. June 18, 1878	Mr. Sumner I. Kimball (Treasury civilian), Chief, Revenue Marine Division. When the Life Saving Service was erected into a separate bureau of the Treasury by Act of Congress approved June 18, 1878 (20 Stat. L. 163), Kimball accepted the post of General Superintendent.
1878 to 1881	Mr. Ezra W. Clark (Treasury civilian), Chief, Revenue Marine Division.
1881 to 1883	Captain James H. Merryman, General Superintendent, Revenue Marine Division. (Register of that period shows he was General Superintendent of building and construction—chief inspector of entire system.)
1883 to 1886	Captain John W. White, Special Duty, Chief, Revenue Marine Division.
1886 to 1889	Mr. Peter Bonnet (Treasury civilian), Chief, Revenue Marine Division.
Dec. 1, 1889 to 1895	Captain Leonard G. Shepard, USRCS, Captain Commandant, Chief, Division of Revenue Cutter Service.
March 19, 1895 to March 27, 1905 (retired)	Captain Charles F. Shoemaker, USRCS, Captain Commandant, Chief, Division of Revenue Cutter Service.
April 1, 1905 to April 30, 1911 (retired)	Captain Worth G. Ross, USRCS, Captain Commandant, Chief, Division of Revenue Cutter Service. (Reference in register shows he retired as Captain Commandant as step in grade. Died March 24, 1916.)
May 22, 1911 to June 30, 1919	Commodore Ellsworth P. Bertholf, Captain-Commandant, Chief, Division of Revenue Cutter Service until 1915 when it became known as U.S. Coast Guard.
Sept. 4, 1919 to Jan. 11, 1924 (Ret)	Rear Admiral William E. Reynolds, first Captain and later RADM Commandant. Reappointed Commandant on Jan. 12, 1923, with rank of RADM effective as of October 2, 1923. He was the first officer to attain this rank.
Jan. 11, 1924 to May 17, 1932	Rear Admiral Frederick C. Billard, appointed Commandant with rank of RADM.
June 14, 1932 to June 14, 1936	Rear Admiral Harry G. Hamlet. Retired with rank of Vice Admiral, Sept. 1, 1938.
June 14, 1936 to Jan. 1, 1946 (Ret)	Admiral Russell R. Waesche. First officer to attain rank of full Admiral.
Jan. 1, 1946 to Dec. 31, 1949	Admiral Joseph F. Farley. Second officer to attain rank of full Admiral. Retired Jan. 1, 1950.
Jan. 1, 1950 to June 1, 1954 (Ret)	Vice Admiral Merlin O'Neill. Made full Admiral on retirement list.
June 1, 1954 to June 1, 1962 (Ret)	Admiral Alfred C. Richmond. Appointed Commandant as Vice Admiral; appointed full Admiral as of June 1, 1960, by Act of May 14, 1960, Public Law 86-474, under which all Coast Guard Commandants thereafter automatically became full Admirals.
June 1, 1962 to June 1, 1966 (Ret)	Admiral Edwin J. Roland, USCG.
June 1, 1966 to June 1, 1970 (Ret)	Admiral Willard J. Smith, USCG.
June 1, 1970–	Admiral Chester R. Bender, USCG.

Index

Page numbers in italics refer to illustrations